"If you have ever dared to dream of living a meaningful life, then you must read this book! *The Entrepreneur's Creed* is not only something you will succeed by; it's something you will want to live by."
    —Ken Blanchard
        coauthor of *The One Minute Manager*® and *Gung Ho!*®

"Your values, your style, and your horizons will be broadened as you read this insightful book. I have been challenged by these stories of people who 'have done well by doing good.' It is refreshing to see so many definitions of success without the dollar sign being put in front of the word."
    —David Burdine
        President, Bethesda Ministries and affiliated companies

"This is a powerful book for those who aspire to entrepreneurial success—but who are beginning to suspect that such success is worth pursuing only within an encompassing framework of ultimate values. The values exemplified in this book take success beyond the superficial into the transcendent realm in which commitment to God and service to people prevail."
    —Dr. Larry Donnithorne
        President, Colorado Christian University

"*The Entrepreneur's Creed* does an excellent job of showing how men and women can aggressively pursue profits and still maintain a focus on serving others. This book shows that profits wisely invested by people with a passion to do good are changing our world in a positive and enduring way. Without God man has no social solutions."
    —Joe Foss
        Former Governor of South Dakota

"Important reading for anyone who wants to understand how values and principles interact in the motivations of successful business people. These entrepreneurs go beyond sound bite simplicity to real value; to wisdom derived from experience reflectively lived and passionately communicated."
    —Gary Ginter
        President of Catalytica, LLC and Ginter VAST Corporation

"Every entrepreneur understands what it means to take a leap of faith. No matter what your faith, this book reinforces the importance of living your convictions in your business life."
    —Harvey Mackay
        author of *New York Times* best-sellers *Swim with the Sharks* and *Pushing the Envelope*

"*The Entrepreneur's Creed* gives the reader many of the lessons learned by successful Christians who have found the secret to a God-honoring marriage of their entrepreneurial skills and their Christian faith."
—Tom Mason
      Executive Vice President, Focus on the Family
      Former Vice President of Marketing, General Motors

"General Norman Schwarzkopf said, 'You can't help someone get up a hill without getting closer to the top yourself.' *The Entrepreneur's Creed* tells the stories of twenty very diverse yet highly successful leaders whose examples and insights can help the rest of us move upward. Enjoy the climb, and keep this rare pocket guide with you."
—Dr. Bruce McNicol
      best-selling coauthor of *The Ascent of a Leader*
      President, Leadership Catalyst, Inc.

"This book raises the bar for all who share the dream of building something new and doing it without regrets. It is all about leadership by character. I was inspired and sharpened by every story, and I know that our students will be as well."
—Stan Oakes
      Senior Vice President, Campus Crusade for Christ
      President, International Leadership University

"Successful entrepreneurs who are committed to Jesus Christ have much to share with us about taking risks for the gospel. Many of the people profiled in *The Entrepreneur's Creed* have challenged and encouraged me personally to continue to dream great dreams."
—Dr. Luis Palau
      President, Luis Palau Evangelistic Association

"*The Entrepreneur's Creed* is an excellent composition of case studies that demonstrate the benefits of applying Christian practices in the world of business."
—Dr. Frank Toney
      Finance Faculty Chairperson, University of Phoenix
      Director, Executive Initiative Institute

THE ENTREPRENEUR'S
CREED

THE
PRINCIPLES
&
PASSIONS OF 20
SUCCESSFUL
ENTREPRENEURS

THE ENTREPRENEUR'S
CREED

MERRILL J. OSTER & MIKE HAMEL

BROADMAN
&HOLMAN
PUBLISHERS

NASHVILLE, TENNESSEE

0-8054-2357-5

Published by Broadman & Holman Publishers, Nashville, Tennessee

Dewey Decimal Classification: 658
Subject Heading: ENTREPRENEURSHIP

Unless otherwise noted, Scripture quotations are from the Holy Bible, New International Version, copyright © 1973, 1978, 1984 by International Bible Society.

Library of Congress Cataloging-in-Publication Data
Oster, Merrill J., 1940–
 The entrepreneur's creed : the principles and passions of 20
successful entrepreneurs / Merrill Oster and Mike Hamel.
  p. cm.
 ISBN 0-8054-2357-5
  1. Entrepreneurship—Moral and ethical aspects. 2. Entrepreneurship—
Anecdotes. 3. Entrepreneurship—Biography. I. Hamel, Mike. II. Title.

HB615 .O85 2001
658.4'21—dc21

00–063099

1 2 3 4 5 6 7 8 9 10 05 04 03 02 01

To Greg Davis, Bruce Duncan, and Aaron Hamel,
early believers in EMT
MIKE HAMEL

To my family, business associates, and customers who have
taught me from real world experiences
MERRILL OSTER

CONTENTS

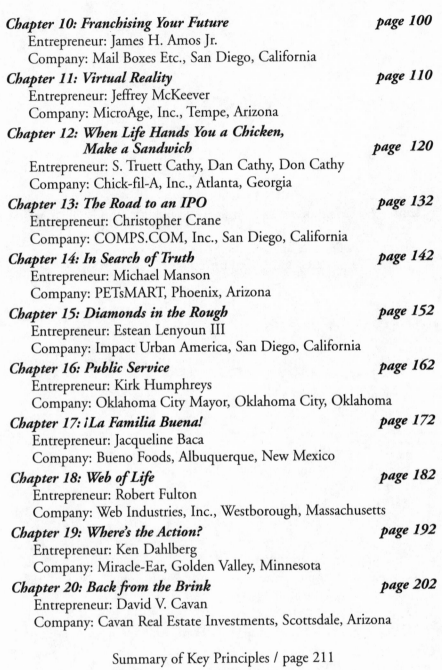

FOREWORD

An *entrepreneur* is someone who takes business risks in hopes of making profits. A *creed* is a confession of faith or system of beliefs. It connotes passion and implies first principles that shape practices. Put the two together and you get a book that combines sound wisdom on how to create wealth with sage counsel on how to be spiritually and ethically grounded at the same time.

The men and women whose stories are recorded in *The Entrepreneur's Creed* represent a broad range of backgrounds, occupations, and management styles. But they share a personal faith in God that is foundational to their public achievements and they share a sense of responsibility to use what they have been given by way of influence and resources to help others.

Their success is a measure of their ability to serve.

"We must never forget," writes philosopher Dallas Willard, "that the riches of this world, whether they are to be regarded as good or evil, are realities that do not just disappear if we abandon them. They will continue to exert their effects. Possessions and use of them will occur . . . . So to assume the responsibility for the right use and guidance of possessions through ownership is far more of a discipline of the spirit than poverty itself. Our possessions vastly extend the range over which God rules through our faith. Thus they make possible activities in God's power that are impossible without them." *The Entrepreneur's Creed* spotlights men and women who are using the wealth created in the free enterprise system.

Our Jesus Christ told his disciples in Luke 16, "Whoever can be trusted with very little [earthly wealth and power] can also be trusted with much [spiritual wealth and influence]." The entrepreneurs profiled in these pages have been trusted with much. By reputation or personal knowledge, I know most of these men and women and can testify to the profound impact they are having through their faithful stewardship.

My prayer is that their example will rub off on the rest of us and society will be changed as men and women practice their faith and express their generosity in their communities. My hearty congratulations to Merrill Oster for his remarkable entrepreneurial skills in building many businesses with great financial success and always with the highest ethical standards. Also for his work with Mike Hamel in giving us such an inspiring and enabling book.

DR. BILL BRIGHT
Founder, Campus Crusade for Christ International
Winner, 1996 Templeton Prize for Progress in Religion

PREFACE

In his song "The River," Garth Brooks encourages his listeners not to "sit upon the shoreline and say you're satisfied," but to "choose to chance the rapids and dare to dance the tide."

"Choose to chance." Take a premeditated risk on something that's far from certain. "Dance the tide." Execute the pattern implied by dance on the agitated surface of everyday life.

These phrases describe most entrepreneurs. Boat People convinced that the traumas of travel are minor compared to the regrets of never having left home. River Rafters who know they can't avoid rocky mistakes but believe they can survive the impact.

If you are among the millions who have chosen to dance the tide in your own boat—or if you are somewhere on board—this book is for you. It contains the compiled wisdom of twenty travelers who have successfully piloted both small and large craft on the currents of commerce.

We want to thank Sue Groves and Joanne Fritz, whose countless hours of typing turned conversations into chapters. We want to thank David Sanford, without whose early and continual help this book would not exist. We also want to thank all the contributors to this book for their willingness to tell their stories and their candor in sharing their lives.

As fellow travelers, we share this book in hopes of encouraging personal faith in a Sovereign God who alone gives purpose and meaning to the whole trip.

MERRILL OSTER AND MIKE HAMEL

INTRODUCTION

According to a 1997 *Inc.* Gallop Survey, 13 percent of Americans (8,500,000 adults) own their own businesses. An additional 13 percent planned to start a business in the next two years, which makes another 9,800,000 people. If you are one of these 18.3 million entrepreneurs, if you are married to one, or if you depend on one for your paycheck, *The Entrepreneur's Creed* is for you.

The Creed tells the stories of twenty entrepreneurs whose companies made or managed billions in revenues in 2000. They candidly share the principles and passions enabling them to live meaningful lives while creating wealth for themselves and others. Their advice on starting and growing businesses comes from the "been there, done that" side of the street and is encapsulated in more than 180 market-proven principles.

This is a book about more than money, though it bursts with insight on how to be successful. This is a book about personal faith and how it relates to public accomplishments. At a time when many are looking for spiritual meaning and purpose in their work, these inspiring stories illustrate the kind of success that doesn't bobble with every drop in the Dow. After all, green is only one color in the rainbow of achievement.

The twenty squares in this patchwork quilt represent a wide range of experience, education, occupation, location, and management style. Each one is a different size and shape. Still, some common threads run throughout: a commitment to God, a sense of calling and purpose in life, a genuine love of people, a willingness to take risks, an aptitude for change, and a desire to learn by doing.

There are no heroes in these pages, just role models. Heroes are so far beyond the pack that it's almost impossible to identify with them. Role models, on the other hand, are people like us—in a little better shape perhaps, but not too far ahead. Examples whose footsteps we can follow because we can step in them.

It's not enough to be out front. These men and women of faith are worth following because they're headed in the right direction.

On your mark,

Get set,

Read!

THE ENTREPRENEUR'S CREED

I believe in God as the First Principle.

I believe in the power of dreams and visions.

I believe in using my God-given aptitudes for excellence.

I believe in work as vocation, as saying yes to an authentic life.

I believe in giving back to build a better community.

I believe in moving beyond success to significance.

I believe in taking calculated risks.

I believe in win-win relationships.

I believe in the value of values.

I believe in lifelong learning.

FOSTER FRIESS grew up in the northern Wisconsin farming community of Rice Lake, where the disciplines and family values laid the base for his success in the mutual fund business. He earned his degree in business administration at the University of Wisconsin. There he was selected one of the ten most outstanding senior men, and there met his wife of over thirty-seven years, the former Lynn Estes.

Together with his role as president of Friess Associates, Foster serves on the Advisory Council of the Royal Swedish Academy of Sciences, which awards the Nobel prizes for chemistry and physics, and on the Humility Theology Advisory Board of the John M. Templeton Foundation. He is also past president of the Council for National Policy and the founder and president of the Life Enrichment Foundation, which makes grants to small, entrepreneurial, faith-based charities with a special focus on the inner city.

Foster has loved hiking, skiing, and hunting since his youth. He has taken up rock climbing and kayaking since moving to Jackson, Wyoming, in 1992. He also claims to be a scratch golfer trapped in a seven handicapper's body. He and Lynn have four grown children, two of whom work at Friess Associates.

Chapter 1

BILLION-DOLLAR MAXIMS

*"Money goes where it's wanted and stays where it is
well treated, and that's all she wrote."*
WALTER WRISTON[1]

In a business that is acutely time sensitive, investment superstar Foster
Friess is available 24-7. "If we don't make the right decisions in minutes,"
says Foster, "it could cost our clients hundreds of thousands, if not millions,
of dollars."

It's a lot of pressure, but in an industry comprised of the quick and the
broke, Friess is adroit enough to have been repeatedly featured in the *New
York Times, Forbes, Investors Business Daily,* the *Wall Street Journal,* and a
host of other financial publications. Kiplinger's ranked his Brandywine
Fund among the top three no-load growth funds in America for the ten
years ended December 1997. In its June 2000 issue, *Money* magazine
named Brandywine to the Money 100, "the best mutual funds you can
buy," for the third consecutive year.

MUTUAL BENEFITS

Earn Trust by Giving It

"To a greater extent than any of the
other great investors," notes the *No-Load
Fund Analyst*, Foster "has created a business involving a number of people who
have been given responsibility for investment decisions . . . . Like most great

Entrepreneur: Foster Friess
Company: Friess Associates, Inc.
  Jackson, Wyoming
Year Started: 1974
Start-up Costs: "two nickels"
2000 Assets under management:
  $9,000,000,000
Employees: 70

investors he is also highly disciplined and has the confidence to act with conviction. These traits and a clear investment process have been essential to the firm's outstanding track record. But the most impressive of all is the successful incorporation of other people into the investment process."[2]

Friess seems to concur with Goethe's insight, "Trust a man as he is and he will remain as he is. Trust a man as he can and should be, and he will become as he can and should be." "We trust our managers to make wise stock picks," he says, "and in turn they treat the money we manage as their own (more than $30 million of it is). I don't look over their shoulders every day or second-guess their decisions. Because all employees own a part of the mutual funds they manage, they have a stake in keeping Brandywine strong. My own mother back in Wisconsin is among our investors. This keeps me on my toes."

If one measure of trust is being granted the right to manage other people's money, Friess certainly passes the test. Some of the most sophisticated institutional buyers and wealthy individual investors in the world place their money in his hands.

Friess, who describes himself as a "recovering perfectionist," admits that trusting people with your reputation is a learned ability. He knows it's easier to grant trust and delegate responsibility when you hire the best people. "Personally, I try to recruit people who are better than I am. And when we look at companies for investment purposes, we look to see what level of associates the CEO has recruited."

In addition to capability, a person must possess a character worthy of trust. "Men of genius are admired," says Arthur Friedman. "Men of wealth are envied. Men of power are feared, but only men of character are trusted."[3]

Take Responsibility for Your Actions

Learning to do chores as a boy prepared the patriarch of the Brandywine Fund family for the later rigors of mutual fund management. "We don't make excuses when our asset values go down. We buy the best companies fitting our criteria, and we don't lay the blame for price erosion on rising oil prices, the strong dollar, or Fed action. I advise everyone starting a business to take responsibility for their decisions—don't make excuses."

In the thirteen years of the Brandywine Fund, no excuses have been needed. Firmwide, assets under management have grown from $1 billion in 1990 to over $9 billion in 2000. An interviewer once asked Foster the maximum amount he could effectively manage. "We have a cutoff of $3 trillion," he quipped. "Seriously, the key to not having too many dollars to invest is keeping our corporate culture lean and mean so we don't develop a bureaucracy."

In his book *Future Edge,* Joel Barker tells of the discovery of "warm" ceramic superconductors by a Swiss physicist, Alex Mueller. "Dr. Mueller was assisted by a young physicist, George Bednorz, who hadn't yet established his reputation. In fact, it was an error by this young man—not setting the oven hot enough—that accidentally provided the first samples of the ceramic compound. Had he been more experienced, he probably wouldn't have made the error."[4] Dr. Mueller capitalized on this error, choosing to ignore the "fact" that ceramic material is an insulator, not a conductor, of electricity. His mistaken idea led to a Nobel Prize.

To Friess, "There's a big difference between perfectionism and excellence. Perfectionism abhors error. It tries to eradicate it and destroy it. Excellence, on the other hand, embraces error, builds on it, and transforms it. We don't have 'mistakes'; we have 'adjustment opportunities.' We don't criticize, but rather we try to encourage excellence by learning from our failures and institutionalizing the way to do things successfully in a companywide Standard Operating Procedures on-line manual."

METHODICAL IMPROVEMENTS

Get the Facts before Making Decisions

The Friess approach to investing is unique, hence his firm's motto: "Never invest in the stock market, invest in individual businesses." In addition to evaluating presentations from companies in which he's thinking about investing, Foster and his team go straight to the firms and check behind the scenes, sometimes even looking for dust accumulating on inventory shelves.

"We invest in individual businesses experiencing dramatic earnings growth and high rates of profitability with sound balance sheets. Our intensive, bottom-up research efforts include calling and visiting top management of target companies, their customers, suppliers, and competitors. We look for companies experiencing at least 25 to 30 percent earnings growth year after year."

Central to Brandywine's success is the strategy of forced displacement. Friess calls it his pigs-at-the-trough theory. "As a kid, I would watch as a hungry pig would nudge up to a full trough, forcing out a satisfied pig. When we identify a company with dynamic growth, we force ourselves to sell the least dynamic company in the portfolio, even if it has growth potential. We sell good companies to make room for great companies."

Go the Extra Mile

Friess credits his parents with inspiring him in two areas. "My father modeled for me what it means to work hard and to go the extra mile. He would rise at 4:30 A.M., drive the countryside buying cattle and return well after dark." His mother taught him frugality and how the little things can count. For instance, he recalls her saving the string from mailed packages for later use. He financed his business degree with savings earned by flipping burgers, picking beans, bailing hay, and corralling Hereford cattle.

Diligence is more than a work attitude; it's a state of mindfulness, a way of life. An instance reported in *Jackson Hole Magazine* tells how, "Last winter as Foster Friess rode the Casper chairlift at the Jackson Hole Ski Resort, he was jolted by an idea that demanded immediate attention. As skiers raced by below, Friess pulled out a cellular phone and instructed his team of associates at the Brandywine Fund to unload one stock and increase the firm's position in another. By the time he reached the bottom of Rendezvous Mountain, his little insight was well on its way to making Brandywine clients $25 million richer."[5]

Don't fret about mixing business with pleasure. Friess remembers Arnold Toynbee's words, "The supreme accomplishment is to blur the line between work and play."

MONITOR YOURSELF

Prioritize for Productivity

Arranging priorities is another critical factor in achieving excellence according to Foster. "At one time I kept track of priorities with index cards. Blue ones for personal things like getting my wife a birthday present; yellow cards for investment research ideas I wanted to check out; pink cards for business responsibilities like signing up a new client. I would arrange these cards by color in rubber bands. On Monday morning I would sort through each pack and pick out the things to do that week and arrange them in order of priority.

"In life you have 'A' priorities, 'B' priorities, and 'C' priorities. If you have fifteen minutes before lunch, you might say, 'I'll knock out two or three "Cs," then I can tackle the "A" list after lunch.' Instead, you ought to take an 'A' priority, cut it into little pieces and work on that before lunch. Don't sweat a 'C' because eventually it will either become an 'A' or become irrelevant. As Peter Drucker says, 'First things first and last things not at all.'"

Monitor Your Proficiency

"When I started out, I kept a time log with five-minute increments. I would write down anytime I changed behaviors. I noted things like reading the *Wall Street Journal*, opening mail, taking a call from a client, even going to the rest room. At the end of the day I marked with a blue pen all the time spent interacting with clients. With a green pen I checked anything involving investment research. I put a red check next to everything else.

"I knew my success came from interacting with clients and making investment decisions. Over time I realized I could grow faster by spending more time in the investment process rather than in the client process. So I tried to shed 'time-sink' clients and those just needing their hands held. I told them, 'I can't make money for you if I'm talking to you all the time. I make money for you by talking with CEOs and CFOs.' I became very careful about the clients I took on. As more and more green ink showed up on my sheet, it has meant more green for my clients.

"At the bottom of my log sheet I had an area asking, 'What are the most important things I accomplished *today?*' Some days I'd make ten or fifteen calls and think, 'Boy, a productive day.' But when it came to writing down the most important thing I accomplished, it wasn't very significant. Other days I'd glance down at the most important thing accomplished, and it may have been something significant like landing a huge client or buying a key stock that eventually turned out well.

"This illustrates the difference between efficiency and effectiveness. You can be highly efficient and very ineffective. Strive for effectiveness first. Efficiency will certainly help, but don't confuse it with effectiveness. We should always be asking ourselves in any moment, 'Am I now doing the most important thing I could be doing?'"

Avoid Meetings Whenever Possible

In his book *Claw Your Way to the Top*, Dave Barry compares "the modern corporate meeting to a funeral, in the sense that you have a gathering of people who are wearing uncomfortable clothing and would rather be somewhere else. The major differences are that: (1) usually only one or two people get to talk at a funeral, and (2) most funerals have a definite purpose (to say nice things about a dead person) and reach a definite conclusion (this person is put in the ground), whereas meetings generally drone on until the legs of the highest-ranking person present fall asleep. Also, nothing is ever really buried in a meeting. An idea may look dead, but it will always reappear at another meeting later on."[6]

Choosing to avoid such unpleasantries, this CEO prefers to spend his time on the road visiting company management and talking to their competitors. "We keep in touch electronically instead of face-to-face whenever it makes sense. Almost all of the interactions within our firm are via e-mail or fax. We are incredibly sensitive to time. I've gotten to the point where I don't get on the telephone except for rare instances, or when I need to talk to a company executive.

"We avoid meetings at all costs, and when we have them, they are in a room with no chairs. Such rare events wouldn't be to transfer information or make decisions but to build rapport, to recognize, or to exhort."

MAKE A DIFFERENCE

Put First Things First and Last Things Not at All

"Put(ting) first things first," explains Stephen Covey, "means operating every day from priorities that flow from your mission, values and goals. It means translating your mission into specific, daily activities."[7] How does this work at Friess Associates?

"In our corporate culture we encourage people to rank priorities of God, family, and clients in that order," says Friess. "We work hard to make sure we can back up each other and help one another so our family needs are not damaged by our work environment. If there's a conflict between a ninth-grader's school play and our annual banquet, there should never be any doubt that the school play comes first."

The priorities he sets for his company are synonymous with his personal values. Foster invests 20 to 30 percent of his time on projects ranging from helping the homeless find jobs, to matching kids with mentors, to advising political leaders. Why such a large investment in others, particularly the less fortunate?

His Conversion to Christ in 1978. Despite growing up in a Christian home, Friess didn't become a follower of Jesus Christ until challenged by a potential client to submit his will to God. "I had a high-level board meeting with myself," says Foster, "deciding who should be the chairman of my board. And I got down on my knees on an October day over twenty years ago and asked Jesus Christ to take control of my life. Accepting him as Lord has made a profound difference."

The desire to obey Christ's teachings motivates Friess's charities to focus on people who are least able to help themselves. Foster says, "When Jesus praised his followers in the Gospel of Matthew, he said, 'You fed me when I was hungry, clothed me when I was naked and visited me when I was in prison.' And they scratched their heads and said, 'Gee, we don't remember doing that.' And Jesus responds, 'Whatever you did for one of the least of my brothers, you did for me.'"

"Foster takes seriously the charge to be a doer of the word, not just a hearer," says John Stapleford, director of the University of Delaware's Bureau of Economic and Business Research. "In all aspects of his life,

Foster puts his convictions into action, and we are the better off for it."[8] His personal and financial involvement includes drug counseling centers, after-school mentoring programs for inner-city youth, teen-abstinence programs, medical vans that aid the indigent, and work programs that help people break free from the welfare system.

Develop Team Spirit through Serving Others

"Foster's obvious concern for the well-being of everyone around him, aside from his business acumen, has forged a special bond among the people who work for him," says Bill D'Alonzo, a vice president and portfolio manager. "He is consistently upbeat, optimistic, really creative, and aggressively competitive, but he's also a team player. He builds relationships among people. He's a strong catalyst for people to motivate themselves."[9]

"Our commitment to a philosophy of serving others before oneself creates a great team spirit," Foster says. "Team decisions are surprisingly selfless. There have been years when the largest bonus did not go to the person with the best raw performance numbers, but to someone who helped another person excel."

Accentuate the Positive

In every area of life, Friess strives to focus on the positive rather than the negative. "I'm motivated by Philippians 4:8, which says, 'Whatever is true, whatever is noble, whatever is right, whatever is pure, whatever is lovely, whatever is admirable—if anything is excellent or praiseworthy—think on such things.'"

In Brandywine Fund quarterly reports, for example, he points out both the top performers and the not-so-great stock picks but writes in such a way as to end on an up note. Instead of emphasizing the errors inevitably made, he's quick to give positive reinforcement to his teammates, which in turn improves team performance.

Choosing to live on the positive side of life's ledger has paid off for Foster. His can-do outlook and genuine love for people inspires fierce loyalty and an assiduous work ethic from everyone at Friess Associates.

His clients would agree that Foster Friess is a rewarding man to know.

SUMMARY OF KEY PRINCIPLES

- Earn trust by giving it.
- Take responsibility for your actions.
- Get the facts before making decisions.
- Go the extra mile.
- Prioritize for productivity.
- Monitor your proficiency.
- Avoid meetings whenever possible.
- Put first things first and last things not at all.
- Develop team spirit through serving others.
- Accentuate the positive.

INFLUENTIAL BOOKS— RECOMMENDED READING

Gardner, John W. *On Leadership.* New York: Free Press, 1990.

Johnson, Paul. *Modern Times.* New York: Harper & Row, 1983.

Muggeridge, Malcolm. *Confessions of a Twentieth-Century Pilgrim.* New York: Harper & Row, 1988.

BOB BUFORD is the former chairman of the board of Buford Television, Inc., an employee and family-owned company specializing in the acquisition and operation of cable television systems. He is founder of Leadership Network, a nonprofit organization created to encourage innovation and entrepreneurship among leaders of large churches and parachurch organizations.

He is also the founding chairman of The Peter F. Drucker Foundation for Nonprofit Management and of FaithWorks, an organization promoting partnerships between marketplace leaders and faith-based organizations.

A graduate of the University of Texas, Bob has held leadership roles with Young Presidents Organization and World Presidents Organization. He has been a moderator of the Executive Seminars of the Aspen Institute. He is the author of *Halftime: Changing Your Game Plan from Success to Significance,* which has sold more than 100,000 copies and of its sequel, *Game Plan: Winning Strategies for the Second Half of Your Life*, both from HarperCollins.

Bob's passions include art, travel, and books. He and his wife, Linda, make their home in Dallas and at Still Point Farm near Tyler, Texas.

Chapter 2

BEYOND SUCCESS
TO SIGNIFICANCE

"Adult life begins when you ask yourself,
'What do I want to be remembered for?' . . .
None of my books or ideas means anything to me
in the long run. What are theories? Nothing.
The only thing that matters is how you touch people."
PETER DRUCKER[1]

"My experience in the television business has taught me a great deal about being a winner in the success game," says successful businessman and social entrepreneur Bob Buford. "But now I realize there are other games, played on other fields. And I've learned there are other ways to win besides dominating the ratings race and piling up the score through increased market share or burgeoning profits."

Bob grew up in Tyler, Texas, where his mother—widowed when he was nine—ran a small radio station. Against great odds she applied for and got a license to operate the first television station in Tyler in 1954. Bob worked there until college. He returned with a business degree and put in what he now refers to as a seven-year apprenticeship. At thirty-one he became the president and chairman of Buford Television, Inc., a year before his mother died unexpectedly.

Entrepreneur: Bob Buford
Company: Buford Television, Inc.
Tyler, Texas
Year Started: 1950 (radio),
1954 (TV)
Start-up Costs: $100,000
1999 Revenues: $78,000,000
Employees: 360

Buford's accomplishments, while significant in business, have been even more pronounced in the social sector. Many would refer to what he's up to as a second career. He prefers to see it as his game plan for the second half of life.

EARLY ACHIEVER

Center Your Life around Specific Goals

Three years after taking the helm at Buford Television, Bob took some time away for an in-depth analysis of his current situation and to plan his future direction. He returned with a half dozen goals that would consume his energies for the next decade. He jettisoned anything in his life that didn't fit into this six-pack.

1. To grow the business at least 10 percent a year.
2. To have a vital marriage to my wife, Linda.
3. To serve God by serving others.
4. To engender high self-esteem in our son, Ross.
5. To grow culturally and intellectually.
6. To figure out what to do with the money I'm making.

This focus increased productivity, as it usually does. Between 1954 and 1986, the company sustained a 25 percent annual growth rate. In the mid-1980s, Buford divested the television stations and moved entirely into the cable business. These and other strategic changes allowed the company to continue its solid growth rate and enabled Buford to sell it in 1999 at a premium. In his early sixties, Bob is now fully engaged in his second half mission for life. Here's how it happened.

Against the backdrop of double-digit achievement, a drama began to unfold. "I started to wrestle with what I wanted out of the second half of my life," Buford remembers. "An unformed but compelling idea gripped me—I should make my life significant, not merely successful.

"Success panic passed through the threshold of my door when I was 44," Bob relates in his book *Half Time*. "It hit me with a blunt object—my slavish devotion to the art of the deal and the thrill of the kill. How much is enough? By this time, the television business had grown beyond our most optimistic projections. As a result, I had long since arrived at—and surpassed—the goals I had established for accumulation of wealth. I had the big house. I had the Jaguar. I could, and did, travel to any place on earth I wished. I had either reached, or surpassed, the plan on most of the rest of my goals as well."

Ask the Right Questions of Success

"Nothing shapes our lives so much as the questions we ask," observes Sam Keen.[2] "Success brought me to a crossroads and forced me to consider a critically important set of decisions before I could take another step," says Buford. "Would I move the finish line forward so I could keep running the race? Would I give myself permission to be open to new possibilities? Could I have a constructive midlife crisis? After success, what?"

The answers became clear during a planning retreat with his wife, Linda, and a business consultant named Mike Kami. Bob grappled with a simple question as profound as it was direct. Mike wanted to know, "What's at the center of your life?" He wanted Bob to define that "one thing," as Jack Palance told Billy Crystal to do in the movie *City Slickers*. Without knowing this, how could Bob strategically plan the future?

"Mike asked me to draw a box and to put inside it a symbol of what was most important to me," Bob remembers. "I had two symbols competing for the space: a cross, representing my personal faith in Jesus Christ, and a dollar sign, representing my skill and satisfaction in earning money.

"I chose the cross, which, ironically, let me be my truest self."

Move beyond Success to Significance

This pick didn't surprise Bob or Linda, but it signaled a turning point for them—the beginning of the second half of the game of life. It represented a commitment to act out a faith present since childhood.

"One of the most common characteristics of a person nearing the end of the first half of life," says Bob with conviction, "is that unquenchable desire to move from success to significance. After a first half of doing what we're supposed to do, we would like to do something in the second half that's more meaningful—something rising above the perks and paychecks into the stratosphere of significance. And significance comes when you find a way to give yourself to God."

This growing desire led Bob to make some major changes in the following months. He didn't sell his business or give away his money and become a minister, but he did redirect his abilities and energies toward different goals.

"For me, the logic of this allegiance led me to stay involved with my business, functioning as a rear-echelon chairman of the board and devoting about 20 percent of my time to setting the vision and values of the company, picking key executives, setting standards, and monitoring performance. The remaining 80 percent of my time was given over to an array of other things, most of which centered on leadership development for churches and nonprofit organizations—serving those who serve others, helping them be more effective in their work."

This orientation grows out of Bob's mission for his second half: "To transform the latent energy in American Christianity into active energy." He has consequently become a social entrepreneur.

SECOND-HALF CAREER

Create and Invest Social Capital

If an entrepreneur, as defined by Peter Drucker, is someone who transfers resources—knowledge, time, capital, and labor—from a state of lower productivity to a state of higher productivity, then a social entrepreneur is someone who creates or multiplies social capital—time, money, and knowledge—and invests it in the community.

Believing we create capacity for what matters, Bob suggests ten disciplines to free up personal resources to be converted into social capital:

1. Delegate—at work and home. You can't do everything and shouldn't try.
2. Do what you do best; drop the rest. Go with your strengths.
3. Know when to say no to OPAs (other people's agendas). You want to pursue your mission, not someone else's.
4. Set limits. Reallocate time to your mission, to your core issues.
5. Protect your personal time by putting it on your calendar.
6. Work with people you like, not with those who drain your energy.
7. Establish timetables. Your mission is important and, therefore, deserving of your attention and care. Transform good intentions into results.
8. Downsize. Get rid of what stands between you and regaining control of your life.
9. Play around a little. Not in the sense that would get you in trouble, but as a way to keep a handle on who's in charge.
10. Take the phone off the hook. Not literally—at least not all the time—but learn how to hide gracefully.

Freeing up assets is only the beginning; wisely reinvesting them for the greatest ROI (return on investment) is the goal. When it comes to investment strategy, Bob says, "I've also learned three cardinal principles from the wonderful coaching of Peter Drucker that guide my work and help me keep control of my life."

1. Build on the islands of health and strength. This is counterintuitive for philanthropy, which tends to help the helpless. Building on strength, however, is a better idea because it builds sustainable experiences and independence.
2. Work only with those who are receptive to what you're doing. Trying to convince people to do what they don't want to do uses four times

the energy required to help someone conceive or implement his or her own ideas.

3. Work only on things that will make a big difference if you succeed.

Work Only on Things That Will Make a Big Difference If You Succeed

Buford is proving as successful in the social sector as he was in business, channeling his time, talent, and money into launching organizations that reflect his interests both as an entrepreneur and as a Christian wanting to make a difference in the world. To date he has helped start four nonprofit organizations:

Leadership Network. Leadership Network is a private foundation created in 1984 to identify, network, and resource senior ministers and staff members of large congregations. The churches represent a variety of Christian faith traditions and are characterized by innovative ministry.

The Peter F. Drucker Foundation for Nonprofit Management. In 1988 Buford, Dick Schubert, and Frances Hesselbein incorporated The Drucker Foundation to help social sector organizations focus on their mission, achieve true accountability, leverage innovation, and develop productive partnerships.

Leadership Training Network. Believing one of the hallmarks of a twenty-first-century church is deployment of the laity in ministry and mission, the Leadership Training Network—begun in 1995—identifies, trains, and provides an ongoing peer coaching network for leaders in local congregations.

FaithWorks. Bob has also launched FaithWorks, a growing network of social entrepreneurs—and those who want to partner with them—with sufficient capacity and a passion to use their resources to grow innovative ventures that meet social needs.

THE DRUCKER EFFECT

Devote Yourself to Lifelong Learning

Buford is a knowledge junkie. "Since learning prepares you to deal positively and productively with change," he says, "it's more important now than ever before. I've had seven jobs in my professional career, and in my current role as a strategic broker, the playing field is constantly shifting. I can't fulfill my mission unless I'm engaged in a fairly systematic and consistent pattern of learning."

The most profound influence on his personal and business life has been his mentor and friend, Peter Drucker, once referred to in a *Forbes* cover story as "the most perceptive observer of the American scene since Alexis de Tocqueville." "I can't think of anything I've done in my second half without consulting with Peter (and there are many things I haven't done because I heeded his advice). I believe everyone should have a mentor—someone at least twenty years older than you—because it helps to talk with someone who has traveled the path before you."

Here are a dozen of the most important lessons Bob has distilled from the father of modern management:

1. The mission comes first. The mission of nonprofits is changed lives.
2. An organization begins to die the day it begins to be run for the benefit of the insiders and not for the benefit of the outsiders.
3. Know the value of planned abandonment; you must decide what *not* to do. Get rid of investments in management ego.
4. Focus on opportunities, not problems. Most organizations assign their best resources to problems rather than opportunities.
5. Management is a social function and has more to do with people than techniques and procedures.
6. People decisions are the ultimate control mechanism of an organization. That's where people look to find out what values you really hold.
7. All work is work for a team. The purpose of a team is to make strengths productive and weaknesses irrelevant.

8. The three most important questions are: What is our business? Who is the customer? What does the customer consider value?

9. Innovation happens outside the mainstream. It must be done in a separate unit insulated from business-as-usual and the tyranny of the urgent.

10. Money follows knowledge. The problem isn't money; it's leadership.

11. Communication is what's heard, not what's said.

12. The answer to midlife burnout and boredom is the parallel career. The most effective road to self-renewal is looking for the unexpected success and running with it.

FINISHING WELL

Write Your Own Epitaph

Woody Allen says he doesn't mind dying; he just doesn't want to be there when it happens. Buford, on the other hand, has already visited his gravesite. His introduction to *Halftime* begins at the end. "None of us knows when we will die. But any one of us, if we wish, may select our own epitaph. I have chosen mine. It is, I should confess, a somewhat haunting thing to think about your gravestone while you are vitally alive. Yet there it is, a vivid image in my mind and heart, standing as both a glorious inspiration and an epic challenge to me."

100X. "It means one hundred times. I have taken it for myself from the parable of the sower in the Gospel of Matthew. I'm an entrepreneur, and I want to be remembered as the soil in which the seed multiplied a hundredfold. It's how I wish to live. It's how I attempt to express my passions and my core commitments. It's how I envision my own legacy. I want it to be a symbol of higher yield, in life and in death."

Thomas Merton once remarked "that in considering any important decision in life, it's imperative to consult your death because, as the English writer Samuel Johnson once put it, 'When a man knows he is to be hanged in a fortnight, it concentrates his mind wonderfully.'"[3]

Find and Follow Your Calling

"From looking at hundreds of people and learning their stories," Buford writes in his book, *Game Plan,* "significance is something embedded deeply within each of us. It's coded into our being. It's something I call 'spiritual DNA.' In the second chapter of the New Testament Book of Ephesians, St. Paul says there is a set of good works prepared for us before we're even born. To me, that's the encoding of a life's work or mission that gets at the true self. Your soul will always be restless until you somehow bring your real-world life in line with your spiritual DNA."[4]

He goes on to advise, "Your second-half mission has been in development for a long, long time. Everything you have done—your successes and failures—have prepared you for a second-half adulthood of meaning and significance. There's no need to reinvent or reform yourself to fit into a calling. The task is to find the calling God has equipped you to fulfill."

Following this inner voice isn't easy, according to writer Gregg Levoy:

We may set out on the road in a great caravan or set out to sea with champagne splattered lustily on our bows, but somewhere out there we come to realize that life is a great devourer, and dreams get swallowed at an alarming rate. Deserted bones litter many a dead beach, reminders of the temptations to which all of us are, always, in danger of succumbing. Furthermore, the soul doesn't care at all what price we have to pay to follow our calls. Our happiness and security and status simply don't matter to it, although our courage, faith and aliveness do. Unfortunately, as Helen Keller once observed, 'There is plenty of courage among us for the abstract, but not for the concrete.' Dreams rarely stir up much trouble, but acting on them does.[5]

Concentrate on What You Do Well

"You may think once I decided what belonged in the box," Buford reflects, "I quickly handed the reins of my business over to a subordinate and walked out the door looking for new dragons to slay. That would have been a big mistake.

"When I sought guidance from two friends, I asked, 'What can I do to be useful?' They responded, 'What does the "I" consist of?' That's an important question because you can't operate out of strengths God hasn't given you. How we act on what we believe grows out of our own history. I think God uses people in their areas of strength and is unlikely to send us into areas in which we are amateurs or incompetents."

Staying with his game metaphor, Bob counsels, "In your first half, you did a lot of things well. Now you need to limit yourself to only a few things to which you will devote your time and energy. There are too many good causes to commit to in this life. If you try to do them all, you'll eventually grow less and less effective in each endeavor.

"Life isn't that easy," Buford concludes. "Stick to the things you know. Play out the knowledge your experience has entitled you to possess. Live out the dreams God has placed within you."

Heed the advice of this player-coach, and when the final whistle blows you, too, will leave the field a winner.

SUMMARY OF KEY PRINCIPLES

- Center your life around specific goals.
- Ask the right questions of success.
- Move beyond success to significance.
- Create and invest social capital.
- Work only on things that will make a big difference if you succeed.
- Devote yourself to lifelong learning.
- Write your own epitaph.
- Discover and follow your calling.
- Concentrate on what you do well.

INFLUENTIAL BOOKS—
RECOMMENDED READING

Bridges, William. *Transitions: Making Sense of Life's Changes.* Reading, Mass.: Addision-Wesley, 1980.

Drucker, Peter F. *The Effective Executive.* New York: Harper & Row, 1987.

———. *The Post-Capitalist Society.* New York: HarperCollins, 1993.

Handy, Charles. *The Age of Paradox.* Boston: Harvard Business School, 1994.

O'Neil, John R., and Jeremy Tucker. *The Paradox of Success: When Winning at Work Means Losing at Life.* New York: Putnam, 1993.

NOEL IRWIN HENTSCHEL is the oldest of ten kids and the mother of seven. From her modest upbringing in southern California, she has gone on to become co-founder and CEO of the world's largest visit-USA travel organization, AmericanTours International, Inc.

Noel received the California Travel Industry Association's prestigious F. Norman Clark Entrepreneur of the Year Award in 1995. She's also been honored as Entrepreneur of the Year by *Hawaii Business* and *Inc.* magazines and as Business Woman of the Year by the National Association of Women Business Owners in 1996. The *Los Angeles Business Journal* calls her one of the top two business women in LA. *Success* magazine named her among the nation's "Top 100 Entrepreneurs" (May 1997), and *Working Woman* featured her in a 1998 cover story and included her in their list of the "Top 50 Business Women."

Inspired by a meeting with Mother Teresa in 1988, she established the Noel Foundation, an organization dedicated to improving the lives of women and children around the world. In 1998, she received the Humanitarian of the Year Award from the California Mother's Association in honor of the foundation's efforts.

In addition to sitting on several boards, Noel cohosts a TV program called *World in Review*, which focuses on international issues. She lives in Los Angeles with her husband, Gordon, and their seven children, five of whom are adopted.

Chapter 3

IT CAN BE DONE!

"The best way to predict your future is to create it."
STEPHEN COVEY[1]

Noel Irwin Hentschel knows how to get things done. More importantly, she knows what she wants to do. "I grew up in a devout Catholic home," she says, "the oldest of ten children. When my mother became ill, I had to assume a lot of responsibilities at a young age. It taught me to depend on God for inner peace and outward strength, a lesson I'm still learning.

"My dad raised us to believe that with God's help we could be whatever we set our minds to." Noel's mind is set on being America's ambassador to the world. Together with her partner, Michael Fitzpatrick, she launched AmericanTours International, Inc. (ATI), which now provides travel services to one million international visitors annually. It's the largest visit-USA producer of tourism to the U.S., generating an estimated $2.8 billion annual revenues for the U.S. economy and an estimated $150 million in company gross revenues in 1999.

FLIGHT PLAN

Say Yes to Yourself When Others Say No

Noel started what would become her career at eighteen. "When I decided to go into the travel industry," she remembers, "I worked in every aspect of it for six years prior to starting my

Entrepreneur: Noel Irwin Hentschel
Company: AmericanTours
International, Inc.
Los Angeles, California
Year Started: 1999
Start-up Costs: $5,000
1999 Estimated Revenues:
$150,000,000
Employees: 200 (400 in season)

own company. It never mattered what somebody paid me but rather what the experience would be. The idea for starting a company grew out of a void in the market. Companies in the U.S. didn't specialize in bringing people *to* America."

"When she was 21," Ivor Davis writes in *Success*, "Noel Irwin Hentschel . . . learned a harsh lesson. 'I was the top candidate for a big sales post at an airline after scoring well on all the tests. But they gave the job to a man, telling me, 'Sorry we think you'll leave us to have kids.' From that moment on, the vivacious businesswoman was to be in control of her destiny. She started her own business, thereby making sure her gender would never again interfere with her ambition. In 1977, at age 24, she scraped together $5,000 in savings, took a $2,000 credit card loan, and opened ATI. 'I maxed out the card to buy the cheapest desks and office furniture I could find, and we were in business.'"[2]

"Working for British Caledonian Airways opened my eyes," she reflects. "No women had advanced very far in the airline industry. They still haven't in terms of being CEOs. I felt the best way to control my own destiny would be to start my own company."

Is it harder for a woman to succeed in business than a man? "Only in the circles run by the traditional 'good old boy's network,'" says Noel. "A woman has a greater challenge in trying to go up the corporate ladder. That's where I see an advantage to being an entrepreneur. Your destiny lies in your capability, not your gender.

"About three years ago I picked up a magazine listing the top one thousand public companies in America. Only *two* had women CEOs! I wanted to make it on my own and not be beholden to someone else. I've always liked the expression, 'I didn't inherit it, I didn't marry it, I earned it.'"

View Your Market from a Different Perspective

"While working for the airlines, I heard numerous requests from people wanting to come to the U.S.," Noel recalls. "About the time I became aware of this demand, I met Michael Fitzpatrick, a veteran in the travel industry. We both realized that with everyone focused on sending Americans overseas, a vacuum existed in the opposite direction."

Not only did Hentschel and Fitzpatrick team up to fill this void; they did so with an international flair. "We brought an international mentality to our new business," Noel says. "Michael is British and has extensive travel experience. I've lived in Israel and traveled throughout Europe, the Middle East, and Australia. We have a broad range of relationships around the world. Because of this, we know the difference between what an Italian wants when coming to the U.S. versus somebody from Singapore or Saudi Arabia.

"In 1977, tours to the U.S. were in their infancy," Fitzpatrick told *Travel Agent* magazine. "The tourism authorities of various American cities used to laugh at me when I suggested that European tourists could be anything more than backpackers . . . . Success came for several reasons. First, we had the right product at the right price for various markets. Then there was the advent of large aircraft flying across the Pacific and Atlantic that brought air fares down . . . and finally, between CNN and the pop music culture, the message of America was transported to households all around the world."[3]

BUDDY SYSTEM

Build on Strategic Partnerships

Thomas Edison once said, "Success is 10 percent inspiration and 90 percent perspiration." Noel and Michael had the capacity for both. "We put in eighteen-hour days starting the company," she remembers, "and were willing to go anywhere to meet with clients to get their business."

Nowhere did they expend more energy than in building partnerships, starting with their own. Noel believes that "having a strong partner, someone you can trust, is very important. My partnership with Michael has been very positive in that we bring different and unique strengths to the company. We have a similar vision and have been successful as a team. Developing a team has been our philosophy from the beginning. We refer to our staff as *team members* instead of *employees*."

Strategic partnerships have been a cornerstone of ATI's business. "Early on we identified key clients around the world," says Noel, "and put together partnerships with them in certain markets. For instance, when we first promoted American motorcoach tours in Germany, which no one had done before, we identified Deutsche Reiseburo and ADAC (the German Automobile Club) as partners. Our risk in offering the tours would be reduced by convincing these two competitors to cooperate. So we went to Germany and negotiated a marketing agreement beneficial for all of us."

Next, Noel and Michael flew to Australia and worked with Qantas Airways and other businesses to develop a consortium to promote tourism from Australia to the U.S. United Airlines chose ATI to serve visitors to the 1984 Summer Games in Los Angeles. The following year ATI started serving Japanese visitors through an affiliation with top tour operators, Asahi and Daiei. In 1987 Cunard appointed ATI as representatives for the *Queen Elizabeth* (the ship, not the monarch).

Expand through Win-Win Relationships

Partnerships that develop into friendships form the foundation for long-term success. Such cooperation is based on integrity, mutual trust, and a belief in win-win relationships. "Every day we are faced with decisions calling for integrity," Noel comments, "decisions involving staff, clients, and suppliers. Your reputation in business grows out of how you respond. Integrity comes from your values, which for me are rooted in my faith in God. I know mentioning God in public makes some people uncomfortable. It's often associated with the radical right. To me, the challenge is living my faith in a way that others can see and inspires them to trust me."

Others have noticed and become long-term partners as a result.

"When we started working with ATI twenty years ago," says Lisa Paul of ADAC Reise GmbH, "None of us thought our business relationship would have grown to be so successful for both of us. What started out as a business relationship, we are happy to say, has grown to a fond friendship with Noel and Michael."

Peter Landsberger of Deutsches Reiseburo says, "ATI developed to become . . . the number one tour wholesaler to the United States in Germany, certainly to a large extent because of the close cooperation, the reliability and high service level, as well as the many innovative ideas of ATI."[4]

TRAVEL ADVISORY

Think Ahead of the Competition

"One of our major strengths has been that we're always one or two steps ahead of our competitors," says Noel, "and in the vanguard of our industry. We are very forward thinking in terms of new ideas and products and how we operate the business."

ATI "firsts" include: a 24-hour multilingual hotline for passengers; foreign-language motorcoach tours; prearranged "fly-drives," which allow visitors the flexibility of traveling at their own pace; and joint marketing endeavors with partners in Germany, the United Kingdom, and Japan. When it comes to products on the visit-USA market, if they didn't invent it, ATI has heavily influenced it.

"What we do best is create ideas, implement them, and cooperate with our partners around the world on selling the United States. If you're doing business internationally, you should avoid becoming dependent on the economy of one country or one continent. That's why we've diversified from the beginning."

Refuse to Take "UN" for an Answer

"We have a distinct culture in our company," says ATI's CEO, "part of which has been to attract creative people who share our philosophy that the word *unable* does not exist. In the travel industry this translates into not saying *unable* on a reservation, which is all too common. Try to make reservations for a hotel or airline and notice how often you get, 'I am sorry, we are unable . . . ' There's even a code for being unable, 'UN.'

"To say the word *unable* does not exist for us means two things. One, we can accomplish anything we put our minds to, and two, we will work tirelessly to confirm every booking we receive. Recently, I started repeating a saying President Reagan had on his desk in the Oval Office: 'It can be done.' I saw this saying on a leather plaque when I visited the Reagan Library, and a copy of it now sits on my desk."

Be Wary of Consultants

Michael and Noel have made their share of mistakes along the way. Near the top of their list they rank spending money on consultants. "I would caution potential entrepreneurs to be careful of consultants," Hentschel says with the voice of experience. "If there ever was a time we wasted money, it was on consultants. These people present themselves as being able to solve all your problems, but if you really think about it, a lot of times you can solve the problems yourself.

"One area where we lacked expertise was in computers. We spent a great deal of time and money trying to find the right consultant to help. Then we decided to handle it internally. We created our own MIS department, hired a CIO, and we now have the most advanced computer system in our industry. This gives us a competitive edge because speed is critical in making and confirming bookings, and speed depends on technology. When we took on this area internally, we ended up getting it done right and much more cost effectively than when we used outside consultants.

"If you *do* bring in a consultant, make sure you're very clear about your expectations and that the consultant lives up to his or her commitment. And always agree up front on a flat fee."

GOOD SAMARITAN

Accept the Responsibilities of Success

Noel believes strongly that "successful people have a social responsibility to give back, to help others. I'm personally driven by the awareness that life's a wonderful gift from God and that I have a purpose. I've been blessed in so many ways and have been able to accomplish so many things with God's help.

"I want to be an active participant in life and make this world a better place. I look up to role models, starting with my grandmothers. Both were hard working and strong leaders. Women like Margaret Thatcher and Mother Teresa have also had a great impact on my life.

"The first time I went to India, my husband and I were among four hundred entrepreneurs attending a Young Presidents Organization (YPO) conference in Delhi. Mother Teresa spoke and challenged us to use the same drive we used to build our businesses to help others. I talked with her afterwards; she hugged me and held my hand. What a transforming moment! It was the closest one could feel to God while still on earth. I felt strongly that this happened for a reason and that I was supposed to do something as a result."

The next year Irwin Hentschel started the Noel Foundation to help needy women and children in cooperation with the United Nations and the Urban League. Since then she has led the charge for private-sector support of humanitarian efforts as a cornerstone to social and economic change.

The goals of the Noel Foundation, according to its founder, "are to help those most in need to help themselves, to turn frustration into opportunity, and to make it possible for the creative entrepreneurial spirit to come alive through action-oriented programs and community projects. And to *never say never* when it comes to turning dreams into reality."

Leverage Your Strengths to Benefit the Weak

Globe-trotting has not only made Noel an astute businesswoman and one of "The Most Powerful Women in Travel," according to *Travel Agent* magazine; it has brought her closer to the harsh realties of the world. She refuses to separate opportunities in business from the responsibilities of helping the destitute.

"I felt I had so much success in bringing business to the U.S. from around the world that part of giving back would be to help women in developing countries become successful. If the foundation can provide them with training and education, these women can earn money for their families and be part of the economic development in their countries.

"That was the beginning focus of the foundation," Noel continues. "When the riots in South Central Los Angeles occurred in the early 1990s, we expanded our focus to include helping children in the inner cities of America by working with organizations like the Urban League and Boys and Girls Challenger Clubs."

Her concern for others led Noel to run for lieutenant governor of California in 1996, but it wasn't an easy decision for her. "I try every day to better understand what work God wants me to do. I look for signs. I pray and ask for direction, then I follow the path I believe he wants me to take. When the opportunity to run for political office came up, I prayed about it a lot with my family. A short time later in New York, I had a chance to ask Mother Teresa for her advice. She took my hand and told me simply, 'If you are able to do it, do it, but don't forget the poor.'"

Noel ran in 1998 and came very close to winning. Based on the outpouring of support she received, this probably won't be her last foray into politics. She cares too much about people—especially the poor—to remain on the sidelines. "My desire to serve in public office is just another way of giving back to the state and country that have given so much to me and my family."

Balance Family, Faith, Business, and Community

Noel is a very busy woman, but she doesn't seem to be out of breath. She does a good job of what she says is "the ultimate challenge for women—*balance*. We must balance our roles at home, in our careers, in our communities, and in our personal relationships.

"The most important part of my life is my family," says this mother of seven. "From them I draw my strength. In my early twenties, within a year of starting my company, I had the unexpected opportunity to make a difference in the lives of three little boys. Although single at the time, I decided to help my sister by adopting and raising Danny, Timothy, and Anthony.

"Some years later I met my husband, Gordon. In time I gave birth to two boys, Nicholas and Patrick, and we also adopted Shannon and Tina— our other boys' sisters—because we wanted to keep all the siblings together. Thus, Gordon and I became partners, soul mates, and together with our seven children, we became a family."

The Hentschel family works together. In addition to Noel's business, Gordon has his own business, and the Hentschels as a family own and operate two resorts.

"To me, success and happiness are tied to being able to do something positive with what we've been given. Everything we have comes from God, and we need to use it to serve him. Money is a tool that gives us more choices in what we can do, but it's not the barometer for gauging happiness or success. That measurement comes from what we do for others. I would like to be remembered as someone who helped make this world a better place.

"And as a woman who never gave up."

SUMMARY OF KEY PRINCIPLES

- Say yes to yourself when others say no.
- View your market from a different perspective.
- Build on strategic partnerships.
- Expand through win-win relationships.
- Think ahead of the competition.
- Refuse to take "UN" for an answer.
- Be wary of consultants.
- Accept the responsibilities of success.
- Leverage your strengths to benefit the weak.
- Balance family, faith, business, and community.

INFLUENTIAL BOOKS— RECOMMENDED READING

Ball, Marshall Stewart. *Kiss of God: The Wisdom of a Silent Child.* Deerfield Beach, Fla.: Health Communications, 1999.

Hesselbein, Frances, and Richard Beckhard and Marshall Goldsmith, eds. *The Leader of the Future.* San Francisco: Jossey-Bass, 1997.

Jones, Laurie Beth. *Jesus/CEO: Using Ancient Wisdom for Visionary Leadership.* New York: Hyperion, 1995.

Ouchi, William G. *Theory Z: How American Business Can Meet the Japanese Challenge.* New York: Avon Books, 1992.

Schuller, Robert. *If It's Going to Be It's Up to Me: The Eight Principles of Possibility Thinking.* New York: HarperCollins, 1998.

Vardley, Lucinda (Mother Teresa). *A Simple Path.* New York: Ballantine Books, 1995.

JERRY COLANGELO checked into the game in 1939 in the Hungry Hill neighborhood of Chicago Heights, Illinois. An outstanding high school athlete, he had sixty-six college basketball scholarship offers and seven professional baseball offers to choose from upon graduation. He ended up at the University of Illinois, where he earned All-Big Ten honors and a place in the Illinois Basketball Hall of Fame.

In 1996 Colangelo ranked as the twentieth most powerful person in sports according to *The Sporting News*. He serves on the NBA's board of governors, the finance committee, and the league's long-range planning committee. In Major League Baseball, he sits on both the legislative committee and the equal opportunity committee.

Also in 1996, Colangelo was named the most influential businessperson in the Valley of the Sun for the third straight year by *The Arizona Business Journal.* He's on the boards of the Phoenix Art Museum, the Greater Phoenix Economic Council, the Phoenix Community Alliance, and the Phoenix Suns Charities. He is vice president of the Phoenix Downtown Partnership and chairman of Southwest Leadership Foundation. He's a former chairman of the Christian Businessmen's Club and former president of Valley Big Brothers.

Jerry enjoys jazz, likes to read, and has fond memories of golf, something he has no time for these days. He and his wife, Joan, make their home in Phoenix, as do their four grown children and eight grandchildren.

Chapter 4

MVP

"Do what you love and you'll always love what you do."
BILLY JOEL[1]

Jerry Colangelo is synonymous with professional sports in the Valley of the Sun. His efforts have made Phoenix one of only eleven U.S. cities with franchises in four major sports. After serving as general manager of the NBA Phoenix Suns from 1968 to 1987, he led a group of investors to buy the franchise (for a then-record $44.5 million) and was its president until 1999. He is now chairman and CEO. *Financial World Magazine* ranked the Suns as the ninth most valuable team in sports and the second most valuable basketball franchise.

In addition to his front-office duties, Colangelo has had two stints as the Suns' coach and owns a 59–60 NBA record. He's the winner of an unprecedented four NBA Executive of the Year awards. He's also been instrumental in the league's WNBA initiative, serving as a founding committee member and president/CEO of the Phoenix Mercury franchise, which led the league in attendance.

But his passion for sports goes beyond basketball. Colangelo became the guiding force for an investment group that landed Arizona's first major league baseball franchise in 1995, the Arizona Diamondbacks. He now serves as the team's man-

Entrepreneur: Jerry Colangelo
Companies: Phoenix Suns and Arizona Diamondbacks
Phoenix, Arizona
Years Started: 1987 and 1995
Start-up Costs: $44,500,000 and $325,000,000
1999 Revenues: N/A
Employees: 135 Suns and 188 Diamondbacks (excluding players)

aging general partner. And then there's the Arizona Rattlers, the 1996 Arena Football League champs.

His efforts to bring professional hockey to the Valley came to fruition when the National Hockey League's Winnipeg Jets—renamed the Phoenix Coyotes—relocated to the America West Arena. The arena, also Colangelo's undertaking, opened in 1992 as the centerpiece for a downtown revitalization process that has made Phoenix one of the most admired cities in America.

FRANCHISE PLAYER

Build a Community, Not an Empire

Jerry Colangelo has a love for the Valley of the Sun, and the feeling is mutual. He's been voted the most influential business leader in Phoenix for five years straight by *The Phoenix Business Journal,* an honor reflecting his commitment to community building rather than empire building. The sense of teamwork permeates everything he does, which is a lot.

"My plate is full," says the busy executive. "The most publicized ventures are the Phoenix Suns and the America West Arena, where we host over two hundred events annually and which is a whole business unto itself. To that I've added the Arizona Diamondbacks and the Bank One Ballpark. Then there are the other sports teams like the Phoenix Mercury and the Arizona Rattlers. We're also the landlords for the Phoenix Coyotes here in the arena. We have a production television company; we have retail stores throughout the Valley and a substantial advertising and public relations company called SRO Communications."

For a business venture to be good for Colangelo, it has to be good for the Valley in particular and for Arizona in general. Don't believe his PR department? Ask his peers, who selected him as Arizona's Master Entrepreneur of the Year. He's also a five-time winner of the *Arizona Business Gazette's* Executive of the Year award.

Trust God's Plan for You

So how did the 6-foot-4 southpaw from Chicago wind up a sports car in the desert?

"Although he played semi-pro after college," writes Ronald Grover in *Business Week*, "it was selling that really fired him up." "He was a hustler all his life," says Frank Narcisi, a friend from Chicago who ran a tuxedo-rental business with Colangelo in the late '50s and early '60s."

Colangelo wanted more out of life and took a risk when offered a chance to get back into the game by Dick Klein, a Chicago consumer marketer. "When Klein proposed applying for what became the National Basketball Association franchise to own the Chicago Bulls," Grover continues, "Colangelo lined up investors to raise the $1.25 million franchise fee. In 1966, when the Bulls took the court, Colangelo was its head scout and merchandising director. Two years later, at 28, he went to Phoenix to put together the Phoenix franchise."[2]

"I react instinctively to life," says Jerry. "It's not programmed; it's not outlined. Many people ask me how I've accomplished all I have. My response surprises them—I have no idea. I just get up every day and go to work. I feel like I'm led to do what I do. I don't have time to think about how I'm doing it. I just go ahead and take the next step. That's a faith I've developed through trials and tribulations, through mistakes and successes. I believe it's part of the game plan God has for me."

Envision the Future You Want to Create

Risking everything on a start-up franchise in a new city, Jerry arrived in the Valley in 1968 with a wife, three young kids, and a few hundred bucks in his pocket. Two years south of thirty, he became the youngest general manager in professional sports. An athlete's work ethic accompanied his faith in God, and soon his career took off.

Colangelo tried to fathom why he was so lucky when other, more qualified people, seemed less fortunate. Hard work certainly played a part, as James Carville observes, "The harder you work, the luckier you are."[3] And Colangelo was no stranger to fifteen-to-twenty-hour days. Yet there was more to it. "One day I came to the realization all this wasn't because of me," Jerry remembers. "It was God's plan."

His trust in God gives Colangelo confidence to lead others into the future he sees. A few years ago he told reporter Ed Graney, "I see things that will blow people's minds. The baseball stadium (Bank One) will be the

America West Arena ten times over. We're taking it to a new level. I see two, three hotels. I see ten million people passing through the stadium and the venues around it per year."[4] And what he's seen is now becoming reality.

Perceiving the possible is a trait Colangelo shares with other dreamers—people like Carl Stotz, the twenty-eight-year-old baseball fan who started the Little League in 1938 while between jobs. Stotz enjoyed playing catch with his two nephews and wanted to turn their make-believe into a real game. He scaled everything from field to equipment down to kid-size and approached corporations to sponsor his first three teams. He got turned down fifty-six times before U.S. Rubber invested thirty dollars for one team. The rest is history.[5]

While Stotz miniaturized the game for children, Colangelo is ratcheting it up for professionals with his $350 million state-of-the-art ballpark, already the new standard in the Bigs. BOB (Bank One Ballpark), as the 48,000+ seat stadium is known, is open year-round and boasts an interactive theme park, children's playground, batting cages, pitching tunnel, museum, restaurants, and a swimming pool complete with waterfall and Jacuzzi. This "mall"ing of America's favorite pastime exemplifies Colangelo's ability to bring professional, civic, and financial interests together in a mutually beneficial partnership.

ROLE MODEL

Embrace the Responsibility of Being a Role Model

Jeff McKeever, another prominent Valley CEO (see chap. 11), reminds business leaders, "You have a responsibility to be thoughtful in what you say because by virtue of your position in life, people take you seriously. You are going to affect their lives, and you ought to give them the benefit of the best wisdom you have. I learned this earlier in life when people would come up to me and say, 'We talked ten years ago and I've been following the principles you mentioned.'"

Colangelo takes this responsibility seriously. "You can't become much more public than I am." (According to the public-opinion firm O'Neil Associates, he's the second most recognizable person in Arizona after former Governor Fife Symington.) "It's a real test for me in terms of my

Christianity and something I have to deal with on a daily basis. Through it all, I've come to understand that the climb up the ladder is a lot more enjoyable than arriving at the top. Once you're perceived as having arrived, attitudes change toward you. You become a target. In spite of this, I have a responsibility in how I carry myself as a public figure.

"For whatever reason, the Lord decided this is where I should be; this is my calling. People are looking to see how I deal with issues in the world of big business as a born-again believer. The incredible exposure that goes with my work gives me an opportunity to assist those groups, organizations, and causes I believe in, especially those furthering the kingdom of God. I'm selective in how I use my name and encouraged when I can help spread the Word of God."

The Jerry Colangelo Lecture Series, sponsored in conjunction with the Pinnacle Forum, is one example of how he seeks to awaken business executives to the importance of the spiritual aspects of life.

Foster Consensus to Improve Competitiveness

Colangelo's faith isn't something he leaves at home. He believes biblical values and big-league management aren't mutually exclusive. One issue he's concerned about is the alienation between players and owners in baseball.

"In deciding to go into major league baseball, I had to do some due diligence. Through this period I identified some reasons why baseball was in the state it was. There had been a total breakdown between ownership and labor management, a total distrust between the two camps. I came to believe the only way to become competitive with the other major league sports again involved bringing these groups together. Yes, there is a collective bargaining process you go through, but philosophically it's important that there's a partnership between the two.

"The essence of the game is healthy competition among teams. But there should be an underlying camaraderie between owners and players because, as the Bible says and history proves, 'A house divided against itself cannot stand.'"

Invest in Good Character

The "new kid" is taking heat from the baseball aristocracy on other issues, like his public statements—and subsequent actions—regarding "acquiring people of character, not characters as it relates to athletes. Believe me," Colangelo emphasizes, "there are plenty of characters out there, and you have to be careful in the selection process.

"I believe people can make mistakes, and you can work with athletes who have made mistakes. You can spend personal time with them, do counseling if necessary. But we're not in the rehabilitation business. We get somewhat of a finished product in the athlete coming into the pro game. He or she has been shaped through experiences in high school and college.

"In the case of the Diamondbacks, when we have opportunities to select people like Jay Bell, who's a strong Christian leader; or when you have a chance to sign a young player like Travis Lee, who is also a strong young leader, these men are the types we want to build our franchise around. We're signing players who will be role models for the team and solid citizens for the community, in addition to playing the game well. Over time you become known as an owner and a franchise stressing good people, and that pays real dividends."

According to manager Buck Showalter, "The team philosophy is to have good people who leave the game better than they went in. We don't want any bad citizens. That doesn't mean I expect a bunch of choirboys. But we want guys our young kids can look up to in adversity. When we bring in a player who's maybe on the fence, the good guys will police them with peer pressure. Still, it all has to show up on the scoreboard."[6]

BIG BUCKS

Pay People What They're Worth

Colangelo's generosity toward players is yet another friction point with some owners, notably George Steinbrenner. "One of the Diamondbacks' most recent signings, which surely must have convinced Steinbrenner that Colangelo was 'a fool,' was that of catcher Jorge Fabregas," writes Pat Jordan in *The New York Times Magazine*. "Fabregas's agent asked for $1.8 million a year for his client, and the Diamondbacks countered with $1.05 million. Fabregas took the Diamondbacks to arbitration, where the Diamondbacks offered him $875,000. The Diamondbacks won, whereupon Colangelo instructed Garagiola (the club's GM) to offer Fabregas a $2.9 million, two-year contract.

"'I called Fabregas and his wife into my office,' Colangelo says, 'and told him what I was going to offer him. He was dumbfounded. He told the media he couldn't believe it. I did it because I wanted guys to want to play for us. And also because I hate the arbitration process.'"[7]

Jerry's emphasis on character and his willingness to pay players what they're worth comes from more than simple altruism. It's sound business. "I'm a stayer," he goes on to say. "Everything I do is long term. When we become competitive, we'll be competitive for the long term. I want a solid foundation. I want to build support in the community. That's why we stress character, work ethic, good people."[8]

Promote Your Values with Your Wealth

Not only is he generous with his players, Colangelo routinely invests in projects and people who will never earn him a cent. He uses his considerable social clout to stir up support for the Phoenix Symphony and other civic organizations. The Phoenix Suns and their foundation, Phoenix Suns Charities, put more than $2 million back into the community annually.

"Money is another gift the Lord has put into my hands," Jerry adds. "As a family, we actively support organizations and ministries helping young people in particular—groups like Young Life, Southwest Leadership Foundation, Big Brothers and Campus Crusade for Christ."

"Money should never be separated from values," says Harvard Business School professor Rosabeth Moss Kanter. "Detached from values it may indeed be the root of all evil. Linked effectively to social purpose it can be the root of opportunity."[9] Wealth, like manure, does the most good when spread around. Colangelo's wealth is helping the desert valley blossom.

HOME BASE

Protect Home Base

"The breakdown of the family today means more children are being raised without the advantage of strong families," remarks this father of four. "In my time, we had extended families like an umbrella around us.

Growing up in a neighborhood of Italian immigrants—my grandparents came to the U.S. at the turn of the century—I understood the value of family. It was a poor community, but no one focused on that. There was great wealth in having your entire family nearby.

"Yet in my immediate family, I didn't have a strong relationship with my father. I've responded in a different way to my children, trying to give them the closeness I didn't have. My wife and I try to model and pass along our faith to our children and grandchildren. To me it's faith, family, and business, in that order. Then comes everything else. It's a challenge to keep the proper balance, but the rewards are worth it. I've been blessed with a great family. I have four married children and eight grandchildren, all living nearby. I simply told my sons-in-law that if they wanted to marry my daughters they had to stay in Phoenix. In return, my wife and I try to create an umbrella of support for them."

Stay in the Game as Long as You Love It

Looking ahead, the Suns' CEO has no plans to slow down. "I'll just keep chugging along doing what I'm doing and enjoying it immensely. I'm focused on making everything I'm involved with better and better. I enjoy watching my family grow around me, especially the grandchildren. I'm trying to have an impact on their lives as they become young adults.

"I'm not thinking about an exit strategy. I know myself well enough to know I need to stay *very* active. I thrive in an environment filled with pressure and stress. So I'll just keep rolling along until I can't roll any longer."

When it's finally time to hang his number in the rafters, how does he want to be remembered? After a reflective pause, he answers simply, "Jerry Colangelo—he believed in God, and he cared about people."

SUMMARY OF KEY PRINCIPLES

- Build a community, not an empire.
- Trust God's plan for you.
- Envision the future you want to create.
- Embrace the responsibility of being a role model.
- Foster consensus to improve competitiveness.
- Invest in good character.

- Pay people what they're worth.
- Promote your values with your wealth.
- Protect home base.
- Stay in the game as long as you love it.

INFLUENTIAL BOOKS— RECOMMENDED READING

The Holy Bible, New International Version. Colorado Springs: International Bible Society, 1973.

Augustine, Norman R. *Augustine's Travels: A World-Class Leader Looks at Life, Business, and What It Takes to Succeed at Both*. New York: AMACOM, 1998.

Briner, Bob. *Business Basics from the Bible*. Grand Rapids: Zondervan, 1996.

W. ROBERT STOVER is chairman of Westaff, Inc., formerly Western Staff Services. A graduate of Waynesburg College in 1942, he later attended the University of Illinois and the Wharton School of Finance. As one of the pioneers of the temporary-services industry, he has authored numerous articles for trade and business publications.

Stover has been as active in the private sector as he has been in business. On the educational front, he is a trustee of his alma mater and has been—or is currently—on the boards of International Students, Inc., The Young Life National Board, San Francisco State School of Business Advisory Board, Fellowship Bible Institute, and Fuller Theological Seminary.

His religious commitments have included service on the boards of The Presbyterian Lay Committee, Mount Hermon Association, Religious Heritage of America, African Enterprise of Capetown, South Africa, and The Luis Palau Evangelistic Association. He is the past chairman of the Oakland Billy Graham Crusade.

In his local community, he supports City Team Ministries, which serves battered women and the homeless. He's also involved with the Boy Scouts of America. Residents of Piedmont, California, Robert and his wife, Joan, have three children.

Chapter 5

EXCEPTIONALLY ORDINARY

"Always remember you're unique, just like everyone else."
ANONYMOUS

Robert Stover describes himself as an average man in an average job with above average goals. What entrepreneur today wouldn't wish to be half as average as the founder of Westaff, Inc., a company with over half a billion dollars in 1998 revenues!

"I have no extraordinary skills," he says, "other than a willingness to work hard." After completing his hitch with the Navy during World War II, Stover went to work as a quality control engineer for Western Electric in New York. The position required a lot of travel. One day while on the other side of the continent, he found the place he wanted to call home.

"I had spiritual and personal reasons for settling in the San Francisco Bay area," Stover recalls. "I wandered into a church in Berkeley and heard the gospel of Christ and responded to it. Shortly after, I decided I needed some stability. I wanted to reorient my life around my newfound Christian values."

But how could he afford to stay in California?

GROWING PAINS

Run with a Concept That's Ahead of Its Time

"About this time," Stover continues, "I read about the man who basically

Entrepreneur: W. Robert Stover
Company: Westaff, Inc.
 Walnut Creek, California
Year Started: 1948
Start-up Costs: $800
2000 Revenues: $700,000,000
Employees: 1,000 permanent
 270,000 temporary

invented this whole temporary business, and with eight hundred dollars I decided to start a service." (Quite a stretch for someone with a B.A. in science and no formal business training.) "I left Western Electric and rented an office on Market Street in San Francisco. I rented a typewriter for three dollars a month to test applicants and started looking for customers."

The concept of temporary employees ran counter to conventional business practice. In those days people worked for a company for keeps, but while most businesspersons accepted the status quo, Stover envisioned the future. "In the mornings I made twenty-five cold calls on businesses, promoting the concept of temporary workers. In the afternoons I interviewed would-be temps, many of them Australian war brides."

This pool of Australian workers compounded the stigma of being temporary with the liability of being new Americans. Yet, when businesses started calling, the brides were among the first to go to work. They were well trained and worked hard. Stover says, "Those from the West Coast might remember our slogan, 'Get a Western Girl.' We became perhaps the first temporary-staffing service of its kind on the West Coast and one of the few west of the Mississippi. As the number of male employees rose, the name changed to Western Temporary Services, then Western Staff Services, and, finally, Westaff, Inc."

That original office has expanded to more than four hundred offices in seven countries, making Westaff one of the leaders in a $50 billion-plus industry growing at an average of 15 percent per year through the 1990s. Talk about catching the wave! Stover doggedly paddled into position for the ride of his life while his peers sunbathed on the beach.

Westaff now supplies a workforce of 270,000 temps to meet the demands of highly competitive businesses, ever-changing global markets, and technically advanced systems. They have diversified to include a wide range of nonclerical temporary help services in the marketing, medical, industrial, technical, and accounting fields.

Solve the Cash Flow Problems That Come with Growth

"Of the one thousand skeptical companies Stover called during the first few months of operation," writes Donna Hemmila in the *Fast Track Quarterly*, "35 percent called back with a staffing emergency. Today businesses no longer view temp workers as a quick fix to a staffing crisis. Employing temporary workers has become a permanent strategy for many companies, one that has turned the staffing business into a high growth industry."[1]

The heavy hitters who swung on Stover's pitch included Bank of America and Pacific Gas & Electric. Bank of America took a couple hundred people for manual stock transfers. On many days scores of requests to Westaff went unfilled. Stover encountered the entrepreneur's dilemma that too much success can be fatal. In need of capital, he soon exceeded the company's small credit limit.

"Early on, our business grew rapidly," he reminisces, "and a problem with rapid growth is the need for working capital. Payroll became our main difficulty. We paid some people daily but most on a weekly basis. Yet we had to wait thirty days for some customers to pay their bills. Big accounts like the government took sixty to ninety days. We needed help with this cash flow problem. Here is where a lot of companies run into trouble. At this point you either sell your business—or at least part of it—or, if you're big enough, you can go to the public market. I opted to try for a line of credit."

Bank on Your Principles

"At this point we were $10,000 overdrawn at the bank. Even though we showed a good profit, the bankers called me in and reviewed our books. They questioned the 10 percent I gave as charitable contributions. 'How can you be giving contributions when you don't have enough money to run the business?'"

A fair question for bankers to ask.

"I explained that as a Christian I believe 10 percent of what I earn is my rent for living on earth. It isn't a gift—it's what I owe as my tithe. We talked about it, and they suggested, 'Why don't you keep track of what that would be for now, and someday when you have enough money you can pay it?' 'That makes good common sense,' I replied, 'but I can't do that because as I understand it, I should be paying my tithe as I earn it.'

"At the end of our discussion, they said they would let me know their decision. I fully expected they would just close us down. I mentally prepared to go into another line of work. A few days later they called and said they felt a young man willing to stick to his principles constituted a good business risk. So they gave us our first line of credit—$25,000. The line of credit has kept growing. Today it's about $90 million."

Ten percent isn't the goal for Stover—it's only the start. "From the beginning, I made a point that at least 25 percent of my personal time, energy, and money would go into religious causes I believe in. For the last decade I've been able to give about a third of my income and, more recently, it's been 100 percent. After all, there are no luggage racks on hearses."

FAMILY MATTERS

Treat Employees Like Family

Westaff today is far from the folksy office of white-gloved war brides Stover opened in 1948. With more than 90 percent of U.S. firms now using temporary help, Westaff alone services more than 100,000 of them each year.

Success hasn't changed Stover's view toward Westaffers. Many business experts would wince at his family attitude. There's no professional distance or keeping employees in their place here. For most of the company's history, he's sent birthday cards to all employees and answered his own phone.

"We've tried to keep Westaff a family-type operation," he says. "For instance, we give benefits to our temporary workers, including a 401K plan with an employer contribution. We make our stock available to them at the same 15 percent discount we offer permanent employees.

"You have to bring in quality people and train them correctly. If you focus on creating integrity, high quality, great performance, and a comfortable workplace, people will stick around. We have many career people who have been with us a long time. I occasionally run into someone whose grandmother worked for us. Much of this has to do with the recognition we give our people, and we feel good about that."

Focus on Creating Value and Let Success Take Care of Itself

Stover definitely believes Westaff is creating value in the world. "One of the great feelings of accomplishment I have is knowing thousands of people in America and hundreds overseas are making a decent living because of us. They are able to raise their families and live their lives in a quality way. Creating jobs is one of the great gifts an entrepreneur can give to the world."

Stover is quick to point out, "We've never emphasized success at any price. While growth hasn't been the preeminent objective, it hasn't been lacking either. We're growing about 10 percent a year. In the half century, only twice have yearly sales dipped lower than the year before."

One reporter notes, "At each stage of expansion, Stover relied on scrappy, old-fashioned business sense to push the venture forward. In 1959 he loaded his wife, three-month-old baby and two-year-old into an Oldsmobile station wagon and headed across the country to sell the idea of temp workers to permanent employment agencies. The four-month-long drive captured 15 to 20 franchises. Stover's first expansion Down Under happened after a former employee moved to Australia and told him about the lack of temp services there."[2]

GOOD HOUSEKEEPING

Make Positive Values a Forethought, Not an Afterthought

"Customers choose us because of a combination of positive values," Robert notes. "Our fairness to the community, our treatment of the people who work for us, our ability to perform, and the way we handle complaints. These things display integrity and shape the company's personality. I believe that across the country we are known as a quality company.

"You have to be fair in everything you do. I ask myself, 'What would Jesus do in this situation? How would he handle it?' Another challenge to an entrepreneur is passing on the positive values of your vision to those who are part of the decision-making process. You also want to be listening to their input because no one has all wisdom. When you have strong people working with you, they make contributions that improve your vision. It's a joint venture, which is exciting."

Stover agrees with Ben Cohen and Jerry Greenfield who believe, "'The business of America is business.' Maybe that used to be the case. But now that business has become the most powerful influence in society, we believe business has to accept responsibility for the welfare of that society and the people in it. Or as we'd say, 'The business of business is America.' . . . In order to maximize its social responsibility a company needs to put its social mission right up front. Values are either a forethought or an afterthought. There's no middle ground. In order to get values in the right place—in order to maintain the balance between your social mission and your financial mission—they have to start out in first place."[3]

Know When to Get Rid of Santa

"The challenge is not to keep from making mistakes," Stover remarks, "but to recognize them and make corrections or adjustments." "When you do anything it's important first to look at all that concerns this action," writes David Steindl-Rast, "how you did it when you did it before, what you did well and what you did not do well, and not to make the same mistake too often. As they say, 'a fool makes the same mistake over and over again, a wise person makes a new mistake every time.' We can't avoid making mistakes, but at least we can avoid the ones we have already made."[4]

"One mistake we made," admits Stover, "involved entering the security business. We supplied guards but didn't arm them. This limited customer interest, so we made a fast exit.

"Some things are OK in themselves, but they can become mistakes if they take you off your main purpose. For example, for many years we were *the* leading suppliers of Santa Clauses. We even manufactured the suits. We deployed hundreds and hundreds of Santas in major stores across the country. But when we evaluated the energy being poured into this small part of our business (less than 1 percent), we realized it diverted us from what we did better. So we got rid of Santa. We disciplined ourselves to cut the things taking us away from doing our basic job with excellence.

"Our focus on the basics means we understand our market segment within the staffing service industry," emphasizes the company's annual report. "Recognizing we can't be all things to all people keeps us clear about our mission."

FATHERLY ADVICE

Have a Realistic Time Frame for Your Dreams

"I would encourage entrepreneurs to have a realistic time frame connected to their dreams," counsels this septuagenarian. "I feel a certain amount of hurry with people today. They read in the media, or see in the movies, young people coming out of school, doing this and that, and suddenly becoming millionaires. If it comes that fast, chances are you don't know how to handle it.

"When you look at business, you should see it as a long-term proposition. America is teaching people to look at business in the short term. That's wrong. A commitment to long-term development gives you the ability to hang in there through the problems. It helps you use your energy well.

"You also have to have a long-term purpose. If you're just in it to make a quick buck, it usually won't work. You'll eventually be found out. You can only build something that's lasting if there is integrity underneath."

"In some ways I'm sorry about building the business slowly," Stover told Tibbett Speer in *Diablo Business*. "Maybe I could have done better, but would we have been better off? We have quite a few people here now who were burned out at other bigger companies."[5]

Pass the Baton Smoothly

Westaff, which went public in 1996, has a plan for boosting sales revenue to one billion dollars. Since going public, they've been acquiring smaller regional and independent temp companies. Although more acquisitions are planned, the major growth at Westaff will come from increased volume at existing operations.

Where is Robert Stover in this billion-dollar picture? In the background.

"I'm winding down. My role is being reduced more each year. That's as it should be."

Don't feel sorry for Robert Stover. While he sold 300,000 shares of stock at the IPO, what he retained still has great value and fluctuates depending on market conditions. Since going public, Stover has given away 75 percent of his stock to various charitable trusts and a family foundation.

"I have no second career in mind except to maximize my involvement with the organizations I serve. America desperately needs moral strengthening. We have a national dilemma because we've turned away from traditional values that have shaped this country—the same values that shaped Westaff.

"I don't care about buildings being named after me. I would like to be remembered as a businessman who tried to live according to the principles and values of Jesus Christ. If I am remembered for that, that will be enough."

Ordinary people can do extraordinary things. "In spite of a lack of special talents, one can find a way to live widely and fully," said Eleanor Roosevelt. "I have had only three assets: I was keenly interested, I accepted every challenge and every opportunity to learn more, and I had great energy and self-discipline."[6]

The same could be said for Robert Stover.

SUMMARY OF KEY PRINCIPLES

- Run with a concept that's ahead of its time.
- Solve the cash flow problems that come with growth.
- Bank on your principles.
- Treat employees like family.
- Focus on creating value and let success take care of itself.
- Make positive values a forethought, not an afterthought.
- Know when to get rid of Santa.
- Have a realistic time frame for your dreams.
- Pass the baton smoothly.

INFLUENTIAL BOOKS—
RECOMMENDED READING

Chambers, Oswald. *Approved unto God.* Grand Rapids: Discovery House, 1997.

Davis, Burke. *Jeb Stuart: The Last Cavalier.* New York: Bonanza Books, 1957.

Kennedy, Paul M. *Preparing for the 21st Century.* New York: Random House, 1994.

Palm, Daniel. *On Faith and Free Government.* Lanham, Mass.: Rowan, 1997.

West, Thomas. *Vindicating the Founders: Race, Sex, Class & Justice in the Origins of America.* Lanham, Mass.: Rowan, 1997.

HERMAN CAIN is the chairman of Godfather's Pizza, Inc., and vice chairman of Retail DNA. He graduated from Morehouse College with a bachelor of science in mathematics in 1967 and earned his master's in computer science from Purdue University in 1971. He has also received honorary doctorates from Morehouse College, New York City Technical College, the University of Nebraska, and Creighton University.

He is the recipient of the 1996 Horatio Alger Award and recipient of the International Foodservice Manufacturers Association's Operator of the Year/Gold Plate Award. Cain has also been honored with numerous humanitarian, leadership, and businessman-of-the-year awards.

Cain serves on several boards including FS Buy, UtiliCorp United, Whirlpool, and the Edmonson Youth Outreach Program. An indefatigable traveler, he logs over 200,000 miles a year as an inspirational speaker and promoter of restaurant-industry causes. Yet he finds time for his hobbies—golf and gospel singing. He is working on his second album of gospel favorites and has written two books, *Leadership Is Common Sense* and *Speak As a Leader*. A native of Atlanta, Georgia, he lives there with his wife, Gloria. They have two grown children.

Chapter 6
FOOD FOR THOUGHT

"Whatever you do, don't play it safe. Don't do things the way they've always been done. Don't try to fit the system. If you do what's expected of you, you'll never accomplish more than others expect."

HOWARD SCHULTZ[1]

Jack Kemp calls Herman Cain "the Colin Powell of American capitalism. His conquests won't be counted in terms of countries liberated or lives saved, but in those things that make life worth living—expanding opportunity, creating jobs and broadening horizons, not just for those he knows, but through his example, for those he'll never meet."[2]

Not bad for a man whose father was once the chauffeur for the CEO of Coca-Cola.

Herman Cain grew up poor in the racially segregated South, but this hasn't stopped him from exerting a powerful influence in every setting he's found himself, from high school to corporate boardrooms. The first person in his family to finish college, he holds two earned—and several honorary—degrees. In 1994 he became the first black president of the board of the National Restaurant Association, the food-service industry's leading trade organization. In 1996 he became the association's CEO and president. Under his leadership, this association made *Fortune* magazine's "Power 25," their listing of Washington lobbying groups with the most political muscle.

Entrepreneur: Herman Cain
Company: Godfather's Pizza, Inc.
   Omaha, Nebraska
Year Purchased: 1988
Purchase Price: N/A
2000 Revenues: N/A
Number of units (2000): 600
Employees: 11,000

Bob Bell, executive director of the Greater Omaha Chamber of Commerce, says that Herman "is the only individual I know who could have been successful as a minister, as a singer, as a businessman, as a politician, or as an educator. He balances all that in a terrific way."

DOWN SOUTH

Open Doors by Exceeding Expectations

In his first book *Leadership Is Common Sense*, Cain chronicles his climb up—and down—and back up the corporate ladder. After college, he worked for the Navy before taking a job as an analyst at Coca-Cola. "At each major decision point in my life and career, my own motivation has come from a deep desire to exceed expectations and make a difference. In doing so, life has been fun, and I've experienced the true secret to success—happiness. If you're happy doing what you're doing, you'll be successful. Success isn't the key to happiness. Happiness is the key to success.

"The color of my skin has never been a barrier to performance or success inside of me, but it's sometimes been a barrier to others around me. Performance that exceeds expectations is the best response to ill-informed attitudes. When I decided to move on from the Navy, I sent my résumé to a number of corporations. The only one that interviewed me was the Coca-Cola Company in Atlanta, my hometown.

"That's when I met Bob Copper," Herman says. "He told me they were interviewing me as a courtesy because my father worked as the chauffeur for the CEO. They really didn't have a job available. I thanked him for being honest, and he took me to lunch anyway, where we got acquainted. Two weeks later I received a call from Coke. Bob told me of his efforts to get approval for another position because I had exceeded his expectations. My work for the Navy and my completion of the tough Master's program at Purdue impressed him. I went back and accepted an offer to become a group manager of management science."

Have a Risk Index "North of .5"

Four years later Herman's boss took a job with the Pillsbury Company and within a few months he recruited Cain. "He told me the job was a risky venture," Cain remembers. "He felt I could help him achieve Pillsbury's aggressive growth objectives. If we succeeded, then other career opportunities might be possible. If we didn't, we could both be looking for new jobs. The possibility of success excited me more than the possibility of failure, so I accepted his offer."

This wouldn't be the last time Cain left a secure job-in-the-hand for a better opportunity-in-the-bush.

"Everyone has a built-in 'risk index,'" Cain told the 1997 League of Nebraska Municipalities Annual Conference, "that's somewhere between zero and 1.0. Only you can determine how much risk you're willing to take, not only in your job but also in your daily life. If your risk index is zero, you're afraid to get out of bed in the morning for fear there might not be a floor there. But if your risk index is 1.0, you'll jump out of an airplane without a parachute, knowing you're going to find one before you hit the ground! There aren't many people with a risk index of 1.0, but good leaders need risk indexes 'north of .5.'"[3]

Cain's index is way north.

UP NORTH

Start Over If Necessary to Climb Higher

Joining Pillsbury in 1977, Cain moved to Minneapolis and rose quickly to vice president of corporate systems and services. He earned a reputation as a guy who could get things done and made it to the thirty-first floor, but his aspirations went higher.

"One day while sitting in my new office, I looked out my window and saw that the inflatable dome of the new Minneapolis stadium had collapsed. I started to feel as if my motivation had also collapsed. Although life was good, something was missing from my job. Then it hit me. I'm bored. As I contemplated these things at the 'old' age of thirty-six, I knew I had to reach for more."

The way up for Cain turned out to be down.

He asked Win Wallin, president of Pillsbury, for help. According to Wallace Terry in *Parade* magazine, Cain told Wallin, "'I can't get to your job from where I am. What do you recommend?' Wallin suggested getting on the operations training track in the company's Burger King division, which could lead to being a regional vice president. 'If you want to run a business, you have to start at the bottom and learn it from the ground up,' he told Cain. It would be an unconventional move. Cain would have to resign his title, give up his company car and nice new office, and forgo stock options to start over, flipping hamburgers with the broiler crew."[4]

"When I left Pillsbury, I never looked back," Cain remembers. "I felt motivated again." Joining Burger King in 1982, Cain completed the two-year training program in nine months and soon became VP of the 450-unit Philadelphia region. In four years the region went from the worst of BK's ten regions to being the best in growth, sales, and profits. Then came the next opportunity. Pillsbury offered Cain, now only forty, the presidency of Godfather's Pizza. The pizza chain wasn't making enough dough. Would he give up another hard-earned VP spot for a shot at being president? You bet. But would Cain be able to make a difference at Godfather's?

Identify and Remove Barriers to Growth

Comedian Stephen Wright tells of an occasion when "a cop pulled me over for running a stop sign. He said, 'Didn't you see the stop sign?' I said, 'Yeah, but I don't believe everything I read.'" Neither does Cain. He's run a few stop signs on his road to the top, choosing to ignore the obvious and believe the possible.

"Others may inspire you," Cain tells Trevor Meers of *New Man* magazine, "but only you can motivate yourself. Since motivation comes from within, you'd better have the right stuff inside. It begins with the love of God inside of me. When you have the love of God, you have the proper perspective of what life is about, and you have a proper perspective of what happiness is."[5]

"Success is also about removing barriers. At the Department of the Navy, I overcame the barrier of 'color' in the minds of others. At the Coca-Cola Company I overcame the barrier of 'low expectations.' At the Pillsbury Company I overcame the barrier of being the 'young whipper-snapper.' At Burger King I overcame the barrier of being the 'old dude' from Pillsbury and the barrier that others wanted me to fail. At Godfather's

I overcame the barrier of disbelief that we could 'yank victory from the jaws of defeat.'"

OUT WEST

Block Out the Unnecessary

The Cain family moved to Omaha, Nebraska, in 1986, and Herman reported to work as the new president of Godfather's on April Fool's Day. He was no joke. Things started to change immediately. Cain pruned the company from more than nine hundred restaurants to about six hundred units, bringing a clarity and focus that had been sorely lacking. Within eighteen months, the business climbed back on the growth track.

Herman preaches that "the ability to block out the unnecessary is the willingness to concentrate your resources for more impact, just as one can deliver a more forceful blow with a fist than with an open palm. Leaders who can't bring themselves to give up the unnecessary for the sake of the necessary don't possess the critical leadership characteristic of focus."

Citing an initial operations meetings at Godfather's as an example, Cain says, "There was no lack of ideas, but as I continued to probe the group with questions, it became clear the concept of focusing on fewer things to accomplish more was difficult at first. By the end of the meeting, the operations people were cautiously enthusiastic about this approach because they'd been the ones most directly responsible for trying to implement too many things too fast. It didn't take long for the entire organization to resonate this idea of focus. By the end of my first month on the job, we had pulled together our first tactical action plan to reinvigorate our quality reputation."[6]

Get Ugly to Get Results

"There is no greatness without a passion to be great," says motivational powerhouse Tony Robbins, "whether it's the aspiration of an athlete or an artist, a scientist, a parent, or a businessperson." Cain's passion for excellence created a laser-like focus early on.

"Sometimes it's necessary to raise the sense of urgency of a key decision to another level. I call this the 'get ugly' principle. Use it sparingly or people will begin to question your emotional stability. During my first sixty days at Godfather's, I asked the director of human resources (HR) when we had last conducted HR audits in our restaurants. An HR audit verifies that all legally required notices are properly posted and that documentation on each employee is available and current. If they're not, we would be subject to fines by the Department of Labor—the last thing on which I wanted to spend money.

"The HR director informed me we had never done HR audits. This happened during a staff meeting with my direct reports, causing me to have a conniption fit (some called it a 'Cainniption'). I directed the HR chief to immediately perform an HR audit on all two hundred company restaurants. I also asked him not to let me see him in Omaha (not even on weekends) until he had finished that task. I excused him from the meeting so he could begin right away. He completed the task in an amazingly short period of time, after which he returned to staff meetings and his other HR duties.

"When I had the fit, it sent a message about the importance of being in compliance with appropriate legal requirements. It inspired other departments to assess their compliance activities to avoid a 'Cainniption.' I'm not suggesting this will work for everyone. It worked for me because of my personality and my leadership style. I tried to do it in such a way that while the message was serious, the HR director understood the problem was the target of the 'Cainniption,' not the person."[7]

But what about when the person *is* the problem? Cain answers, "I learned from Peter Drucker that if you have a people problem, then fix it immediately. There's a compassionate way to do this, but procrastinating on the action—once you are convinced you have identified the person as the barrier to their own success—isn't fair to the organization or to the individual."

Partner with People You Trust

Despite Cain's heroic turnaround performance at Godfather's, it became apparent by the fall of 1987 that Pillsbury planned to sell the chain. Cain and Ron Gartlan, his executive vice president, "got a crazy idea. If they did decide to sell GPI, then we would buy it. I asked Ron if he'd ever dreamed of doing something like that and he said, 'Nope.' I said, 'Neither have I, but how hard can it be? I've bought a house before.' We soon found out just how hard it was.

"Ron and I felt prepared for the challenge of putting nearly everything we owned on the line and betting our futures on our belief in the Godfather's concept, but most importantly, betting our futures on our belief in ourselves. In terms of our beliefs about life and family, Ron and I are as alike as two people can get. In terms of our personalities, we're as opposite as you can get. I'm considered an extrovert, and Ron is more of an introvert. I've never found a podium I didn't like, and Ron has never found one that he did. Having complementary skills, abilities, experiences, and even personalities between business partners is something one can hope for but rarely find. Ron and I are one of those rare occasions. Even more rare is, on top of it all, we're also friends."

IN CONTROL

Believe in Yourself and Others

Herman Cain's speech at the company's second "all systems" meeting in 1988 proved momentous for several reasons, including the announcement that earlier that day he had signed the deal on the management-led leveraged buyout. This excited his audience because the move promised continuity of leadership for Godfather's.

He went on to outline the beliefs underlying his confidence for leading the company into a bright future. "First, I believe our Creator put us on this earth to make a difference—to make a positive impact on the lives of other people, whether that's in our family, our business, our church, or our country.

"Second, I believe in myself. When I came to Godfather's, some of my then-colleagues at Pillsbury and BK did not believe we would be here today, talking about our future. I came without a golden parachute, and I came committed to prove the skeptics wrong. And we did! My belief in myself is inspired whenever someone says, 'Can't,' 'Maybe,' 'I doubt it,' or 'Yeah . . . but,' because as Henry Ford said, 'Whether you believe you can or you believe you can't, in either case, you're right.' I believe in myself because I do not believe in those small, thornless, motionless, spineless, parasitic creatures called 'yeah, buts.'

"Third, I believe in other people who are winners. Winners are the right people with the right stuff in the right game with the right coach . . . . I believe in other people who are winners, even though it makes me vulnerable to disappointments and sets me up for letdowns. But believing in other people who are winners is a necessary condition for success."

Give God the Glory

Cain is a hard worker and he has a lot to show for it. Yet he's quick to point out that his success is a gift from God. "The secret of my success is no secret," he says, "it is my belief in Jesus Christ. I give God all the glory for what's happened in my life. I believe we are put on earth to make a difference and to serve others. As I have prayed and sought God's guidance, he has given me some wonderful opportunities to do that. It's not because I'm so great but because he's so good."

This faith isn't something Herman keeps to himself. "When I get up I don't take my beliefs off," he tells Evan Gahr in *The American Enterprise*. "That's like coming to work with one shoe. Some people think prayer is separate from business, but I don't." After speeches in which he mentions religion, Cain says people tell him, "I liked the fact that you referred to your faith." "I say in a loud voice, 'Why are you whispering?'"[8]

Cain has risen from a blue-collar household to the oak-paneled boardrooms of corporate America. "Success is a journey, not a destination, and my journey has exceeded my expectations," he says with a ton of deep gratitude. "I have never looked back, and I have never ridden in the back of the bus because I never wanted to miss my next destination."

SUMMARY OF KEY PRINCIPLES

- Open doors by exceeding expectations.
- Have a risk index "north of .5."
- Start over if necessary to climb higher.
- Identify and remove barriers to growth.
- Block out the unnecessary.
- Get ugly to get results.

- Partner with people you trust.
- Believe in yourself and others.
- Give God the glory.

INFLUENTIAL BOOKS—
RECOMMENDED READING

Gingrich, Newt. *To Renew America.* New York: HarperCollins, 1995.

Kelly, Kevin. *New Rules for the New Economy: 10 Radical Strategies for a Connected World.* New York: Penguin, 1999.

Kouzes, James M., and Barry Z. Posner. *Credibility.* San Francisco: Jossey-Bass, 1993.

Peppers, Don, and Martha Rogers. *Enterprise One to One: Tools for Competing in the Interactive Age.* New York: Doubleday, 1999.

Powell, Colin. *My American Journey.* New York: Random House, 1995.

Ries, Al, and Jack Trout. *Marketing Warfare.* New York: McGraw Hill, 1986.

NORMAN MILLER went to work at his father's Interstate Batteries distributorship after graduating from North Texas State University in 1962. He soon moved to the corporate headquarters in Dallas, where he worked as a traveling salesman. His leadership qualities drew attention, and in 1978 he became president and chairman of this fast-growing company.

In 1991 he turned the role of president over to his brother, Tom. As chairman, Norm continues to focus on strategic planning, advertising, and promoting. The job change also gives him more time for his other passion, evangelism. He has shared his faith in Jesus Christ everywhere from country clubs to prisons. He and his wife have a ministry called Front Line Outreach (FLO), which has taken them on short-term mission trips to Russia, Bulgaria, Albania, Mongolia, and countries in Central and South America.

Never far from automobiles, Miller is cofounder of the Interstate Batteries Great American Race, which has become the world's richest old car race. Beside his involvement with NASCAR and NHRA, (National Hot Rod Association), he enjoys snow skiing and fishing.

Miller is board chairman of Overseas Council International and serves on the boards of Dallas Theological Seminary and Dallas Seminary Foundation. He and his wife, Anne, have two children and five grandchildren and live in Dallas, Texas.

Chapter 7
RECHARGED!

*"Business leaders of all persuasions and temperaments can
legitimately use their companies to stimulate social change . . . . Keep in
mind that social consciousness should not—indeed must not—obscure the
importance of disciplined management and sound business practices . . . .
To do social good you must first and foremost perform well."*
JIM COLLINS[1]

Norman Miller woke up one morning in March 1974 with a terrible hangover. As he lay there, head throbbing, the terrible truth overwhelmed him.
He was an alcoholic. He had lost control of his life. It was a frightening
realization!

Looking at Miller today, you wouldn't suspect the personal demons he
has faced and conquered—alcohol among them—on his road to success as
the chairman of Interstate Batteries of America. Norm didn't start the company, but he helped make Interstate the number-one replacement battery
in North America. He assumed the president and chairman roles in 1978
after working under his mentor and company founder, John Searcy, for sixteen years. Miller and his team have
grown the business to more than 300 distributors and 200,000 dealers. Battery
sales have steadily improved from
250,000 in 1965 to over 12 million in
1998.

Entrepreneur: Norman Miller
Company: Interstate Battery
System of America, Inc.
Dallas, Texas
Year Started: 1952
Start-up Costs: $75,000
1999 Revenues: $480,000,000
Employees: 500

Miller's trip to the top wasn't always a
joy ride. Personal problems roiled around
in the backseat almost from the start.

DIVINE PIT BOSS

Conquer Your Personal Demons

Miller's success in business can't be separated from the battles he's fought and won in his personal life. "I grew up in Galveston, Texas," he remembers. "My dad ran a Gulf service station and garage, so I've been around cars for as long as I can remember. I guess that's how I ended up in the battery business.

"I inherited something else from my dad—drinking. I started in junior high. I gravitated toward people who drank a lot. This proved easy to do in Galveston because it was a big party town. I made it to college and went on drinking and partying. Somehow I graduated, got married, and ended up in an Interstate distributorship with my dad and brothers in Memphis, Tennessee.

"In 1965 I went to work directly for Interstate," Norm continues, "moving to the national office in Dallas. Being in sales put me on the road more than eight months that first year. This freed me up to keep on partying while selling batteries.

"One morning in March 1974, I woke up with a terrible hangover after a night of drinking-as-usual. I called in sick to work. As I lay there in bed, the truth overwhelmed me. I was an alcoholic. I had lost control of my life. What a frightening realization. I blurted out in desperation, 'God, help me! I can't handle it!' He heard me and took away my compulsion to drink. That marked a new beginning for me."

That Friday night Norm went to an Alcoholics Anonymous meeting and soon started attending a Bible study. In his autobiography *Beyond the Norm*, he tells what happened next. "I understood I could no longer avoid making a decision about Christ's claims. So for two hours one night following a Bible study, I sat and talked with the leader, Myles Lorenzein, about my questions. Finally, at midnight, I accepted Christ through prayer, just as the Bible teaches."

Include Spirituality in the Workplace

Interstate's chairman is vocal about his faith and candid about the spiritual dimension of his company. This has drawn national attention. The

March 13, 1995 cover of *U.S. News & World Report* shows Miller, Bible in hand, next to the headline "The Rise of the Christian Capitalists."

"A band of spirited—and spiritual—entrepreneurs is changing business, politics and religion in America," the article opens. It goes on to describe a day at Interstate. "The men have shown up for work an hour early—at 7 A.M. on a Monday—for their weekly, voluntary Bible study group. They are drivers and salesmen, younger fellows mostly, wearing the company-issued, green-pinstriped shirts. The Bible study is conducted with the blessing of Interstate chairman Norman Miller, a born-again Christian who believes religion not only belongs in the workplace but is an essential part of business success . . . . 'I need to be faithful to Jesus 100 percent of the time,' declares Miller. '*And* that includes my business.'"[2]

Miller isn't alone in believing spirituality belongs in the workplace. "Most people would agree that there's a spiritual part of our lives as individuals," write Ben Cohen and Jerry Greenfield of ice cream fame. "Yet, when a group of individuals gets together in the form of a business, all of a sudden they throw out that whole idea. We all know as individuals that spirituality—the exchange of love, energy, kindness, caring—exists. Just because the idea that the good you do comes back to you is written in the Bible and not in some business textbook doesn't make it any less valid.

"Most companies try to conduct their businesses in a spiritual vacuum," they continue. "But the reality is, we'll never actualize our spiritual concerns until we integrate them into business, which is where we spend most of our time, where our energy as human beings is organized in a synergistic way, and where the resources exist that allow us to be at our most powerful."[3]

Interstate has taken the unusual step of hiring a company chaplain, Henry Rogers. He provides counseling to employees and organizes financial contributions to spiritual and social causes.

WINNING STRATEGY

Seek Divine Guidance

"Our executive team has a regular prayer time each week," says Miller. "Urgent prayer requests for employees, their families, our distributors and customers are put on our E-mail prayer chain. We open our functions with prayer, including our national seminars. We ask God to direct us in how to be witnesses and yet sensible in business. We ask for wisdom as to where to put the people we have. If we need to hire, we ask him to bring us the right people. If they happen to be Christian, fine; if not, that's fine too. We've committed our company's success to God, but we don't think of Interstate as a Christian company."

William Pollard, chairman of the ServiceMaster Company, doesn't believe there is such a thing as a Christian company either. But, like Miller, he thinks faith has an important place together with profit in business.

"When you walk into the lobby of our headquarters in Downers Grove, Illinois," he writes in *The Soul of the Firm*, "you see on your right a curving marble wall that stretches ninety feet and stands eighteen feet tall. Carved prominently in the stone of that wall in letters nearly a foot high are four statements that constitute the objectives of our company: 'To honor God in all we do; To help people develop; To pursue excellence; To grow profitably.' . . . Few people find fault with our commitment to a set of principles. Frankly, it is the 'God language' that raises eyebrows.

"For us, the common link between God and profit is people," Pollard continues. "But we live and work in a diverse and pluralistic society, and some people may either question the existence of God or have different definitions for God. That is why at ServiceMaster we never allow religion or the lack thereof to become a basis for exclusion or how we treat each other professionally or personally. At the same time, I believe the work environment need not be emasculated to a neutrality of no belief."[4]

Faith is a growing factor in business in America. McGraw points out in the article quoted earlier that "nearly half of all small-business owners in the nation identify themselves as born-again believers." Still, personal piety won't save you from poor business practices. Being a Christian doesn't mean being a patsy. "I've done business with General Motors, Walt Disney, Goodyear, and others," says Tom McRae, Miller's friend and former business partner. "But I have yet to do business with anyone who's tougher at the negotiating table. He gets a nickel out of every penny."

Pay Attention to Promotion and Packaging

What did Miller do differently after taking the wheel at Interstate? "I can take credit for boosting our advertising and promotion," he reflects, "because Mr. Searcy didn't believe in them. I want at least $2.50 in return for every advertising dollar we spend.

"There's a tendency for companies in our market not to be concerned with the aesthetic value of the product. A black battery goes under the hood and nobody gives a flip. I feel it's important to have an appealing battery, to make it look attractive, modern, and powerful. This gives us a leg-up on the generic 'black battery' people.

"At one point, things started getting real competitive. Competitors started chopping at our market share by lowering prices. Interstate operates on a reasonable profit. To cut prices would mean operating at a level below a minimal return for our equity and investment. If we have to go lower than a reasonable profit point, we might as well find another business. There's no sense in being both tired *and* broke! So my deal became increasing the value of the package rather than cutting the price. It's paid off for us. Not only are we profitable, our market share now hovers around 14 percent, triple what it was when I took over."

Consolidate Around Prime Strengths

"Staying on focus is another thing we did right," Miller continues. "We stayed after penetration in our foundational business and didn't follow tangents. Every time we started doing something else I'd say, 'Wait a minute! We can still sell more batteries.' This is our core business. It's where we're known. It's where our strength lies. We had opportunities to go international, and we would think about it. But then we would realize we could still do more in Chicago and Philadelphia and Pittsburgh and Dallas.

"Don't forget who butters your bread. I teach our people that the better we do in a market, the better we *can* do. The more you've got—if it's based on a quality program—the more you should be able to get. Build on your success."

POLE POSITION

Excel at Helping Others Excel

Over 200,000 dealers sell Interstate Batteries, and Miller has spent a lot of time thinking about how to make them successful. "If you're trying to get people to do something—and you want a higher percentage of them to do it well—you should do everything *you* can, leaving them to do only what you can't. Say your objective requires twelve steps. If you can do nine of them, do the nine and leave them just the three to focus on. The more you free others up to do their jobs, the better they will perform.

"Another thing, we provide a support base that goes beyond mere information. We have an entire accounting package, P & L statements, receivables, everything. This helps minimize the efforts our distributors have to put into their financials. We supply sales materials and training help. We provide advertising, promotion, and inventory control information. We furnish every kind of support. It's good for both of us.

"The utilization of assets is a strong suit of mine," notes Norm. "I'm not just talking about hard assets, but things like relationships, attitude, and history. The key is understanding your assets and using them together to accomplish your objectives. People often miss the chance to leverage their assets by not seeing the whole picture."

Synergy is working together so that "the whole becomes greater than the sum of the parts," as Aristotle put it in the fourth century B.C. The parts, according to Miller, include intangibles like reputation, attitude, and company personality. Miller cites Interstate's involvement in auto racing as an example. "It's good for the company but it also gives us a platform for outreach to the racing community. We didn't get into the racing ministry to further the business, but by doing so it helps the business through strengthening personal relationships.

"When properly understood, synergy is the highest activity in life," says Stephen Covey. "Synergy is the essence of principle-centered leadership. It catalyzes, unifies, and unleashes the greatest powers within people."[5]

Crank It Up 15 percent, but Don't Electrocute Yourself

"Certain givens exist in life," Miller emphasizes, "and work is one of them. There are fixed costs we have to pay. I ask our people, 'If 100 percent is excellent, what percentage do you have to do to keep a good job?' Most everyone agrees it takes a 70 to 85 percent effort. So if a 75 percent performance is necessary just to keep your job, what about excellence?

"Excellence, let's say, is a 90 percent effort, making the difference between being excellent or mediocre as little as 15 percent. Achieving excellence means cranking up your efforts, your thinking and your attention to what you're doing by 15 percent. What's 15 percent of a forty-hour workweek? Six hours. An hour and fifteen minutes a day can mean coming in twenty minutes early, leaving twenty minutes late, and only taking half an hour for lunch. A small price to pay for excellence!

"Excellence is attainable. Those things everybody wants—money, recognition, a good job—are only a little more effort beyond where you may already be. I tell our people, 'Go the extra mile. Get there early, stay late, and pay attention to what you're doing.' That's how we built Interstate."

However, Miller isn't preaching workaholism. "I'm not talking about killing yourself. At Interstate, our mentality is in the fifty to sixty hour-a-week range, not the eighty-plus a lot of people put in, and that includes travel.

"John Searcy's philosophy rubbed off on me. I'm sure we could have grown faster, but we agreed that just because the opportunities existed we weren't going to push ourselves into one high-risk move after another. If something wasn't within a reasonable work ethic and a sound financial risk-reward approach, we chose not to pursue it."

It takes more time and effort at the start of a new business or project but watch out that scheduling "exceptions" doesn't become the "rule." Jesus once asked, "What does it profit a man if he gains the whole world but loses his soul."[6] The word *soul* is the same as the word for *life*. If you spend your life in the pursuit of things, you'll lose your soul in the process—one hectic day at a time.

VICTORY LAP

Reallocate Your Time to Pursue Your Passions

Around 1988, Miller started losing his passion for business. "I steered the ship by my gut. I knew what to do, but I didn't want to do it. I felt God moving me on. So over the next few years I transitioned the presidency over to my brother, Tom, and flip-flopped from 80 percent business and 20 percent ministry to 20 percent business and 80 percent ministry."

What's he doing with his free time? Would you believe making movies? "My wife and I formed a production company called Norann Entertainment, and we're shooting our first movie right now in California. It's called *The Joy Riders* and stars Martin Landau and Kris Kristofferson. I've always enjoyed watching movies, especially with my family. But with the sex and violence, it's gotten to where I'm uncomfortable with what's available. I thought, *Why doesn't somebody make decent movies I can watch with my wife or grandchildren?* I kept talking about it and one day God seemed to say, 'What about you?' I met some movie people who felt God speaking to them in the same way, so we formed this company. If the first movie goes well, we'll do another one and see where God wants to take us."

Relish Playing on the House's Money

Norm Miller is having the time of his life these days. "I've been walking with God long enough to know he is a God of goodness and kindness. We humans have a tendency to relate his goodness to how life is going, but I know he's going to bathe me in his favor, no matter what my circumstances are.

"We just came in second at the Daytona 500. We are thankful, but if we had come in twenty-fifth, God's goodness is still on us. I know people who say, 'that's easy for you to say, being so successful.' But remember, I hit bottom as an alcoholic. I've also had other painful struggles along the way.

"Still, much of my life has been playing on the house's money. If you've gambled, you know when you're playing on the house, you're playing with money that's not yours. Say you start with $100 and win another $200. You put your $100 back in your pocket and play on your winnings—the house's money. That's how I feel. God has blessed me beyond my expectations and I'm so thankful I don't know how to express it."

"Life is truly a ride," says Jerry Seinfeld. "We're all strapped in and no one can stop it. When the doctor slaps your behind, he's ripping your ticket and away you go. As you make each passage from youth to adulthood to maturity, sometimes you put your arms up and scream, sometimes you just hang on to the bar in front of you. But the ride is the thing. I think the most you can hope for at the end of life is that your hair's messed, you're out of breath, and you didn't throw up."[7]

Norman Miller hasn't thrown up in a long time. He's having quite a ride, and it's not over yet. Imagine all this fun, and heaven too!

SUMMARY OF KEY PRINCIPLES

- Conquer your personal demons.
- Include spirituality in the workplace.
- Seek divine guidance.
- Pay attention to promotion and packaging.
- Consolidate around prime strengths.
- Excel at helping others excel.
- Crank it up 15 percent, but don't electrocute yourself.
- Reallocate your time to pursue your passions.
- Relish playing on the house's money.

INFLUENTIAL BOOKS— RECOMMENDED READING

Anderson, Neil T. *Victory Over the Darkness*. Eugene, Ore.: Harvest House, 1997.

Carnegie, Dale. *How to Stop Worrying and Start Living*. New York: Simon & Schuster, 1984.

McDowell, Josh. *More Than a Carpenter*. Wheaton, IL: Tyndale, 1980.

Stanley, Charles. *How to Handle Adversity*. Nashville: Thomas Nelson, 1992.

JOHN BRADLEY has almost thirty years of consulting experience in educational, business, and private counseling applications. His specialty is coaching senior executives and managers in career redirection for themselves and their personnel. He also does training for independent consultants in the career advancement field.

John earned the bachelor of arts in speech and communication from the University of California at Davis and the master of divinity from Western Seminary in Portland, Oregon, where he started the IDAK Group in 1980. He also conducts a maximized productivity seminar for small businesses, which equips managers and employees to achieve maximum productivity through the use of their natural strengths. Bradley hosts a weekly radio broadcast, "The Weekend Business Coach," targeted at entrepreneurs.

A gifted communicator, John is author of *The IDAK Career Match System*, *Switching Tracks*, *The Complete Job Search Guide*, and coauthor of *Discovering Your Natural Talents*. He has written scores of articles and is in demand as a conference speaker and radio-TV talk show guest.

John enjoys the great Northwest by sailing, canoeing, sea kayaking, and wilderness hiking. He volunteers his time on service projects for churches, nonprofit organizations, universities, and seminaries. Together with his wife, Cathy, and two children, he makes his home in Portland, Oregon.

Chapter 8
MASTERING YOUR CRAFT

"Every person is born for a purpose. Everyone has a God-given potential, in essence, built into them. And if we are to live life to its fullest, we must realize that potential."

NORMAN VINCENT PEALE[1]

As a consulting firm, John Bradley's IDAK Group is part of a growing segment of the entrepreneurial population. According to Dun & Bradstreet, there were 285,896 consulting firms in the U.S. in 1999. Of these, 238,876 were business-and-management consulting firms. Eighty-nine percent of these firms gross under $500,000 a year.

IDAK is among the 80 percent of American companies with fewer than twenty employees, yet they have consulted with some of the most recognized names in American business, including the American Red Cross, AT&T, the Federal Reserve Bank, Hewlett Packard, Honeywell, and New York Life. IDAK's founder, John Bradley, has also worked with professional athletes, nonprofit organizations, educational institutions, and government agencies. His corporate clients range from Fortune 500 giants to small, family-owned businesses.

Entrepreneur: John Bradley
Company: The IDAK Group, Inc.
Portland, Oregon
Year Started: 1980
Start-up Costs: $0
1999 Revenues: N/A
Employees: 7 (training and materials used by more than 600 independent consultants)

COMPETENT
TO COUNSEL

Convert Insight into Income

Some entrepreneurs come up with better ways to make or market existing

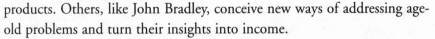

products. Others, like John Bradley, conceive new ways of addressing age-old problems and turn their insights into income.

"Back in the 1970s," Bradley remembers, "career counselors worked only in universities and high schools. The profession was in its infancy. I worked at the University of California, Davis, as a career guidance counselor for three years. When I decided this was what I wanted to do as my profession, I left the university to go to seminary. I had the technical skills, but I wanted a philosophical and theological understanding of what makes people tick.

"While in seminary, I got a job as director of career guidance for a nearby college. I began my private practice as a joint venture with the college. Three years later I decided to go into business for myself. With the help of a financial partner, I started the IDAK Group in 1980.

"IDAK means 'unique identity,'" Bradley explains. "We are a career consulting firm combining personal counseling with career advancement technology. Our approach to helping individuals and corporations achieve peak performance is based on the belief that natural talents identify a person's most productive strategies and determine the type of work they do best. We help people discover and develop these innate aptitudes."

Grow by Trial and Error

"As I counseled individuals, I began thinking, *I could do this a lot better by creating my own career assessment instrument.* I convinced some people they could make money from my idea, and we set up a limited partnership. It flopped, and we went in the drain $20,000. We had to recoup and start another limited partnership. This one succeeded because of what we learned the first time out."

As Henry Ford put it, "Failure is only the opportunity to begin again more intelligently."

"Successful entrepreneurs allow themselves the freedom to fail," John says with the timbre of experience. "Not everything you try will work. Even if you're instinctively suited for what you're doing, you still have to learn by trial and error and trial and error and trial and error. Soon you start collecting what floats from among the stuff that sinks. You also find out what does *not* work for you.

"You have to believe in what's driving you because nobody else knows what you're after. You probably don't even know the whole of it yourself. Abraham Lincoln lost six elections before becoming president. Thank God he believed in what he was trying to accomplish. Eventually something clicks and you go, 'Wow! I've discovered something no one taught me!'

"If you have a conviction that what you want to do is worthy, you may have to sell the idea to others to raise the needed capital. You will definitely need to sell it to employees who join you and may have to take less pay than they could get elsewhere because they believe what you're doing is worthwhile."

Give Away Razors to Sell Blades

Turning an idea into a business, or a concept into a tool, isn't easy, but it's the key to what Bradley did. Creating a tangible product incarnates theories and ideas into something others can see—and buy. And if you're going to charge three or four times more for it than for similar products, as Bradley does for the Career Match System, it had better be good.

"We raised $500,000 in development funds, spent 1983 doing research, and came up with the Career Match System. Our instrument measures three different categories of aptitudes," Bradley points out, "whereas most instruments—like the Strong Campbell's—measures only one dimension. We've identified fifty-four natural talents and categorized them into communication talents, relational talents, and functional talents. These talents apply to every conceivable job, career, and type of work. Our system has a database of sixty thousand job titles. Most other instruments use a database of no more than two thousand titles."

Although possessing a superior product, John says, "We weren't equipped to market the instrument like a publishing firm markets a book. We lacked the know-how, the money, and the networks. We tried and failed miserably. (We later learned if it takes one dollar to make it, it costs three dollars to sell it.) So we decided to market a counseling service and sell the instrument as part of that. We gave away razors to sell razors blades. We taught people how to set up and manage a career guidance practice and then sold them our product. Through this process we created our own market."

MASTER YOUR CRAFT

Maximize Your God-given Talents

"The key to the IDAK approach is the belief that every person wants to do something significant in his or her life," says Bradley, "to make a meaningful contribution so their lives really matter. To help people find that most significant position, job, or occupation, IDAK focuses on finding people's innate abilities, not learned skills, college degrees, or personal passions. The assessment of natural talent is at the heart of our system.

"Natural talents are innate capacities that lead to intuitive job performance. I believe they are God given, but you don't have to accept this in order to benefit from them. It's like seeing beautiful flowers. I'm saying God made them, but you don't have to agree to enjoy them.

"Natural talents are set apart from other important aptitudes," Bradley continues, "such as work skills, personality traits, interests, and values. They are the best predictors of future 'best match' career options. When these talents are applied in one's work, they unleash a power substantially greater than what comes from the traditional motivations of paycheck, status, security, or benefits. Learned skills acquired by training or work experience can't adapt to new job duties. They don't grow or naturally upgrade.

"My lifelong quest is to understand how natural talents impact productivity and fulfillment in achieving goals. At IDAK we develop ways of appraising talents and enabling people to use them in making career decisions. At the outset no instruments existed to diagnose talents, so we designed our own that is computer scored and tied into a large database."

Strive for a 60-40 Balance at Work

John believes that "for individuals to reach peak performance, they must be using their inherent aptitudes for excellence. Discovering and developing them is like mastering a craft. To be in their proper niche, a person should be 'doing their craft' 60 percent of their time on the job. The other 40 percent will be comprised of red tape, hassles, and boring details.

"The best you can realistically expect from your job is that 60 percent of what you do will draw on your talents. If you accept this is about as good as it gets, you can relax and avoid the unrealistic search for a big payoff. Yes, some may be doing better than this, but only after they've settled into a compatible occupation and groomed it over time to fit them.

"Accepting a job is like buying a house," says John. "To enjoy the benefits of ownership, you also agree to put up with the responsibilities of maintenance. Look for 60 percent 'ownership' and 40 percent 'upkeep.' If the percentages are better, that's a bonus. If they're worse, you're going to be frustrated."

Steve Tsuchiyama, who interviewed Bradley for a medical trade journal, put it like this. "It is such an obvious maxim (which is probably why it's violated so often): your work should make the best use of your natural talents. Yet, the core of unhappy departments, unhappy workers, poor productivity and quality, may not be bad people, but rather misplaced talents. Not to say that laziness and apathy do not exist. The real tragedy, though, is the person who never gets to display his or her talents. Everyone loses."[2]

Initiate, Develop, or Die

An entrepreneur by virtue of his "initiator-developer" talent, John says, "I need something new every eighteen to twenty-four months. So I had to create an organization giving me the ability to innovate and develop. I'm like a building contractor. I've got to have a new building under construction every two years as opposed to managing a shopping center I've already built.

"A naturally gifted entrepreneur, after finishing one thing, wants to get the next thing started. But he has these people who are part of the first effort and who just want stability and security. At this point two choices loom: sell the shopping center or find someone to run it and go build a retirement home using the revenues generated by the center. If the organization doesn't let the entrepreneur go build his retirement home, he's dead. It's over, and he'll either quit or get fired."

Can an entrepreneur turn into an operations (day-to-day) manager?

"No way," says Bradley. "That's like trying to turn a buffalo into a domestic bull. As long as there's something exciting and dynamic to be done, the initiator/developer is gung-ho. But the minute he or she starts maintaining, depression can set in, and it's time to find a new vision or move on."

THE CREATIVE WAY

Engender Loyalty That Overcomes Incompetence

As a consultant, Bradley gets paid to learn things from others. "I just did a project for a well-known, major computer manufacturer that involved closing one of their plants. As a company, they do the miraculous in getting maximum productivity out of their average managers. They've learned how to get ordinary horses to perform like stallions.

"This became apparent when we shut down the plant," reports John. "Ninety-five percent of the employees stayed with them rather than go elsewhere. It was so good they wouldn't leave. How did the company create this loyalty? I'll tell you. They have such phenomenal benefit packages and working conditions that people will tolerate average managers just to get a good evaluation report so they can move ahead in the company.

"I marveled when I assessed their senior managers. Less than half had the natural talent to do their jobs. Still everything hummed right along. This place produced despite the management bottleneck. The military has done the same thing. They teach, 'you salute the uniform, not the person.'

The brilliant people—the ones making money for the company—aren't being hindered by less-than-brilliant supervisors."

Scott Adams, creator of Dilbert, puts it this way, "The underlying fact that prompted me to write *The Dilbert Principle* is that it takes less brains to be a manager than to be the people who are managed. For example, it takes a big ol' brain to write a computer program with a revolutionary new data encryption algorithm. A much smaller brain is needed to command that programmer to write status reports justifying his value . . . . There are already millions of highly skilled employees being managed by people who aren't nearly as bright."[3]

Attract Creative Problem Solvers

"The other secret of this world-class company's success," Bradley continues, "is they've learned the importance of two natural talents: creativity and problem solving. They have a healthy sprinkling of these talents at all levels, including at the top. It percolates up from their hiring at the college level. They've figured out in their recruitment how to find instinctively creative people who are also intuitive problem solvers.

"You can spend your time doing the thing right, that is, perfecting the process, but then you may not be doing the right thing. This manufacturer doesn't have that problem because they have lots of people who keep asking, 'Are we doing the right thing?' When something isn't working well, managers and employees know it before it ever gets to the point of smelling. Once something dies, everyone knows. There's a positive aura within the company because these 'creatives' are always asking, 'Why do we do this? Why do we do that? Can we do it another way?' The creative talent consistently thinks outside the box."

Make Benefits a Sticking Point

Bradley works on building such loyalty at IDAK. "The people working here feel like this is a big part of their lives," he believes. "The company becomes part of them. They're more than employees—they have say-so. They are honored as craftsmen and craftswomen.

"I believe in the value of gain-sharing developed by Bob Doyle in his book *Gain Management*. There is involvement at all levels on decisions affecting the profitability of the company. Everyone has access to our financials, and they give input on management decisions. We use a management team approach rather than a president leading by fiat. I can't spend more than one hundred dollars without team approval. That's by my own choice. I don't like it, but I prefer the loyalty I receive from our senior staff."

Another example of IDAK's sensitivity is the company's approach to time. "We are heavy into flextime because when we found the people we liked, they wouldn't come to work full time. We're better off having them with flextime than not at all. It's a struggle in terms of efficiency, not having them on site constantly, but we get higher-caliber people by being flexible."

INTERIOR DESIGN

Listen to Inside Experts

Years of consulting have made Bradley an expert listener, a skill every businessperson should cultivate. "If someone is working in her niche and using her natural talents—say as a machine tool operator—she should be considered an expert and given authority and stature when it comes to machine tools," says IDAK's CEO. "However, she wouldn't have stature in marketing or finance. When it comes to communication and decision making, each person can speak with authority as the 'expert' in his craft. A good boss will listen to each one with credence and respect.

"This kind of respect isn't based on titles," he continues, "but on people's aptitudes. The manager's job is to equip them to do what they do best. Max DePree has documented this type of work culture in his book *Leadership Is an Art*. At Herman Miller, Inc.—one of the best-managed Fortune 500 companies—DePree proved this unique culture of empowering people can fit in today's competitive business environment."

Calibrate the Human Factors as You Grow

Most businesses that fail do so at the point of peak sales. To help companies avoid the pitfalls of growth, Bradley talks about a set of key *factors* a CEO or president has to gauge as a business adds more personnel. "It's important not to let growth overcome what you and your key people do well," Bradley warns.

"When it comes to managers, you have to consider the Stretch Factor and the Mix Factor. The Stretch Factor is how many warm bodies doing the same thing can be added to a manager's responsibilities before the manager flames out. The Mix Factor is how many people can be added who are doing distinctly different things.

"Think of the Stretch Factor like adding cars to a train," John elaborates. "How many can the engine handle before it's overloaded? Think of the Mix Factor as increasing the number of tracks. How many lines can the track manager coordinate before chaos takes over? The Stretch Factor is much easier to implement. The Mix Factor, if not understood, can cause burnout.

"When it comes to employees, you have to assess the Flex Factor and the Growth Factor. The Flex Factor considers how an employee adjusts to change. Does she see change as a positive thing or something to be resisted? The Growth Factor measures how a person is improving at what he does. Is he growing in the mastery of his craft?

"The Flex Factor and the Growth Factor are important when you hire people because if the job changes a year from now—which is highly likely—you need to know if they will still fit and be productive."

Have a Knack for What You Do

Much of business is about competition, but Bradley is an entrepreneur who makes money by helping others become successful. He's good at what he does. You might say he has a knack for it. "It's so rewarding to watch people, from executives to reentry homemakers, finally learn where they function best and move on to reach their full potential. That's my passion."

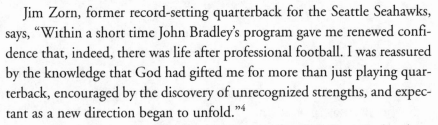

Jim Zorn, former record-setting quarterback for the Seattle Seahawks, says, "Within a short time John Bradley's program gave me renewed confidence that, indeed, there was life after professional football. I was reassured by the knowledge that God had gifted me for more than just playing quarterback, encouraged by the discovery of unrecognized strengths, and expectant as a new direction began to unfold."[4]

Zorn's reference to God doesn't surprise Bradley. "I believe God endows each of us with natural aptitudes. But just identifying these and aligning them with our work can still leave us feeling empty inside. Submitting ourselves to God through Jesus Christ according to the Bible empowers us to find a purpose in life that goes beyond the physical. It literally makes all the difference in the world.

"I'm right where I ought to be," John concludes, "and doing what I do best. I'm at peace with myself. I'm living out what I think is important in life as a person, a boss, a husband, and a father. To me, this is success."

Who can argue with that?

SUMMARY OF KEY PRINCIPLES

- Convert insight into income.
- Grow by trial and error.
- Give away razors to sell blades.
- Maximize your God-given talents.
- Strive for a 60-40 balance at work.
- Initiate, develop, or die.
- Engender loyalty that overcomes incompetence.
- Attract creative problem solvers.
- Make benefits a sticking point.
- Listen to inside experts.
- Calibrate the human factors as you grow.
- Have a knack for what you do.

INFLUENTIAL BOOKS—
RECOMMENDED READING

Belasco, James A., and Ralph C. Stayer. *Flight of the Buffalo, Soaring to Excellence, Learning to Let Employees Lead.* New York: Warner Books, 1994.

Buckingham, Marcus, and Curt Coffman. *First, Break All the Rules: What the World's Greatest Managers Do Differently.* New York: Simon & Schuster, 1999.

DePree, Max. *Leadership Is an Art.* New York: Doubleday, 1989.

Doyle, Robert J., and Paul I. Doyle. *Gain Management, a Process for Building Teamwork, Productivity & Profitability throughout Your Organization.* New York: AMACOM, 1992.

Drucker, Peter F. *Managing for Results.* New York: HarperBusiness, 1964.

ROSEMARY JORDANO was born and raised in Norwood, Massachusetts. She attended nearby Wellesley College and graduated magna cum laude in 1984 with degrees in economics and psychology.

After a short stint as an investment banker, she ventured to England to earn a master's in developmental psychology from Oxford in 1986. She completed her trifecta with an M.B.A. from Stanford in 1989.

Jordano has received the Boston Jaycees' 1998 Top Ten Outstanding Young Leaders Award, the Pinnacle Award for Achievement in Business from the Greater Boston Chamber of Commerce, the Stanford Graduate School of Business Leadership Award, and the 1997–1998 Leading Women Award from the Patriots' Trail Girl Scout Council.

She is a member of the Regis College Board of Trustees, the Dana Farber Leadership Council, the Women's Health Leadership Forum at Brigham & Women's Hospital and the national board of Jumpstart. She has also served on the advisory board of the Kids Fund of Boston Medical Center.

Rosemary learned to love golf while at Stanford. She also enjoys reading—a book a week—running, and just being outdoors. She makes her home in Boston.

Chapter 9

KID STUFF

"A teacher affects eternity."
H. B. ADAMS[1]

The Bureau of Labor Statistics estimates that more than 41 million women of childbearing age work outside the home and that the number will reach 44 million by 2000. "Without child care services of some sort," reports the *Boston Globe*, "millions of workers in all levels of jobs would have to abandon their children or their jobs . . . . Child care is a market force of its own. Once viewed as little more than daily baby-sitting, the industry has blossomed into one of the fastest-growing markets in the country, estimated at $30 billion a year."[2]

One entrepreneur carving her own niche in this nascent market is Rosemary Jordano, founder of ChildrenFirst Inc., which specializes in the development and management of backup child-care facilities. The company serves more than 220 blue-chip corporate clients in ten cities. Since opening in 1992, they have maintained an impressive 99 percent customer-retention rate.

HEAD START

Use Your Head to Follow Your Heart

"I grew up with an immigrant mentality," says Rosemary, whose parents were first- and second-generation Italian immigrants. "My family is Catholic and I attended Catholic schools growing up.

Entrepreneur: Rosemary Jordano
Company: ChildrenFirst Inc.
Boston, Massachusetts
Year Started: 1992
Start-up Costs: $1,000
1999 Revenues: $11,000,000
Employees: 165

I have always been mindful of my faith, and my relationship with God gives me the strength I need to do what I have to do. This became very real to me when my mom got breast cancer. I learned that it's in the middle of your worst fears that you can find the grace you need through prayer."

Another component of Rosemary's immigrant mentality is her work ethic. "You work hard, you get things done, and you contribute, not just to your family but to the community at large," she says. This ethic translated into academic excellence and a position with a prestigious firm in New York after college. But deeper fires burned in Rosemary that money could not stoke.

Some younger entrepreneurs have an overwhelming sense of personal mission. For Rosemary Jordano, it was improving child care. After graduating from Wellesley College, she went to work as an investment banker at Merrill Lynch. "I knew it wasn't the right thing for me on day one," she says. Within a year Jordano was studying developmental psychology at Oxford University. She observed child care settings and classrooms in both England and the United States, and found severe shortcomings: unqualified teachers, too many children per class, weak academic programs, and dismal classrooms. "They just weren't the best places for children."[3]

Jordano brought her burden for children back to the States. "I returned from Oxford and went back into investment banking for six months to get the money to go to Stanford. While there I wrote the business plan for a child-care company. I wasn't interested in business for business' sake, but I also didn't want to pursue my plan in a nonprofit setting or in a government agency.

"I had an excellent mentor, a professor named Irv Grousbeck. He said of my vision, 'This is not a business; this is a social service.' That challenged me to come up with a business model that would work in the marketplace."

Find a Way around Roadblocks

"I believe nonprofits have something beneficial for society," says Rosemary, "but I wanted a for-profit market solution for the well-being of children. I realized in my second year at Stanford that business is a powerful vehicle for getting things done if you have a good concept and a great team to execute it. In coming up with a workable model, the constraining factor proved to be the parents' ability to pay. Then I realized that getting the corporations involved would give me the resources to supply the highest caliber care for children."

By targeting businesses rather than families as clients, Jordano cleared a major financial hurdle on the road to viability. Corporate coffers would pave the way to higher ground.

"Most successful new businesspeople do not start out in life thinking that this is what they want to do," says Paul Hawken in *Growing a Business*. "Their entrepreneurial ideas spring from a deep immersion in some occupation, hobby, or other pursuit. Spurred by something missing in the world, the entrepreneur begins to think about and envision a product or service, or a change in an existing product or service. The entrepreneur is often the first one to spot the opening, and if things work out that person will have a successful business."[4]

Pull the Trigger When Passion and Profit Line Up

Hawken goes on to advise, "Your best idea for a business will be something that is deep within you, something that can't be stolen because it is uniquely yours . . . . Your business must be an extension of who you are and what you are trying to learn and achieve. You know what you want to replace, improve, or change."[5]

"Some people are meant to run businesses, any business, because they are just good managers," Jordano believes. "And then there are people who are meant to pursue a business because of its underlying value. For me, I have a profound belief that children deserve excellence because each child is unique, precious, and unrepeatable. That's what drives me. One of the words we use a lot at ChildrenFirst is *diligence*. It comes from a Latin word meaning 'to love or to pursue with passion.'"

Passion and profit aren't mutually exclusive reasons for starting a business, but an entrepreneur should understand their relationship to each other in her own thinking. The crosshairs of success are personal passion and market need. When they intersect, the entrepreneur pulls the trigger.

HOMEWORK

Prepare Your Supply Lines in Advance

"I moved back to Boston to be near family after I graduated from Stanford. I worked in child care for almost three years before starting ChildrenFirst. I financed the start-up with personal debt by using my credit cards. But early on I approached three colleagues I had worked with in banking and said, 'I'm going to start this company. If it's successful, I would like you to invest in it. I don't want your money now because you are my friends. My relationship with you is more important than this business.'

"By the end of the first year, we had attracted some prestigious clients, which helped validate the concept of backup child care and our ability to provide it in a quality way. I went back to these friends and asked them to invest now, and they came in, supplying us with a few hundred thousand dollars of working capital. A year and a half later we did a significant round of financing, raising three million dollars to become a national company. In 1999, Lazard Capital Partners and Carousel Capital invested sixteen million in growth capital to accelerate the expansion of our national network.

"The trouble with doing something right the first time," as someone put it, "is that nobody appreciates how difficult it was." Things have gone well for Jordano, but that doesn't mean it's been painless. "I've made every mistake you can possibly make," she admits. "The good news is, I haven't made the same one twice.

"I would advise anyone starting a business to always raise more money than you think you need. And always hire talented people sooner than you think you'll need them. It's worth investing in your team ahead of time and letting the business grow into them. Hire people who are way smarter than you. Just make sure their values are in sync with yours."

Document the Need for Your Services

Do your homework if you want to convert potential clients into paying customers. CFI can point to sources such as Cannon Consulting Group's 1996 survey of three hundred chief executives, 72 percent of whom said worker absenteeism would be greatly reduced with the availability of backup child care.

"Backup child care is the number one issue for employers and employees according to a 1997 poll of more than 2,000 companies by *Working Mother* magazine," says Rosemary. "According to a 1997–98 Hewitt Associates study of 1,020 employers, 15 percent now offer backup child care, compared with 5 percent about five years ago, while 10 percent say they have full-time centers."

Jordano and her staff know the numbers. They have written and spoken on child-care issues around the country, including at the White House. "An estimated 60 percent of American children under age six are in some form of child care," Jordano and Marie Oates wrote in the *New York Times*. "But who takes care of them and how? . . . At a recent White House conference, much attention was focused on a Yale University study that reported that 86 percent of the reviewed child care centers offered poor to mediocre care."[6]

In contrast to the dark backdrop of poor care and inadequate coverage, ChildrenFirst paints a solution as bright and simple as the decor of their centers. Here's how it works, according to Nancy Rivera Brooks in the *Los Angeles Times*. "Employees make a reservation, show up at the appointed time with children (ages three months to twelve years) in tow, and proceed to work, happy in the knowledge that their kids are being entertained at a site that is more secure than most bank vaults and by a teacher, who more likely than not, holds an advanced degree.

"All of our teachers have associates, bachelors, or masters degrees. Ninety percent have bachelors and 40 percent have their masters. This is not at all typical in child care."[7]

SHOW AND TELL

Specialize in Win-Win Solutions

Improving a client's bottom line is a sure way to increase your own. Jordano states that "absenteeism due to a breakdown in child care is expensive. The Child Care Action Campaign estimates such absences result in $3 billion in lost productivity for businesses. Furthermore, according to the *Journal of Accountancy,* losing a valued employee to child-care problems costs a company up to 200 percent of the departing employee's salary to find a replacement.

"We are able to show our clients a return on investment within the second quarter of their participation with us," ChildrenFirst's CEO boasts. "The availability of backup child care boosts productivity, enhances employee morale and loyalty, and gives companies a measurable advantage in recruiting and retaining highly valued employees. One 1998 estimate by Work Family Directions, a leading work-life consulting firm, states that every dollar invested in backup child care yields three to four dollars in productivity.

"In a survey of more than five thousand employees at a variety of Fortune 500 companies, 96 percent of respondents reported that corporate-sponsored child-care services enhanced their job satisfaction." The numbers show that putting dollars into backup child care makes sense. Another set of numbers tells why ChildrenFirst has such a high client-retention rate.

Set the Standard for Excellence in Your Field

ChildrenFirst annually surveys their parents, and more than 98 percent of them peg their satisfaction as exceptionally high. "The number one reason our clients—children, parents, companies—are so satisfied is the outstanding quality of our teachers," says Rosemary. "The investment we make in our people gives us a competitive advantage. We don't see how little we can get away with or ask what are the minimum standards required. Instead, we sell our clients a vision of excellence for children."

This is all the more distinctive when compared to the lack of professionalism and inadequate training among child-care workers in general. In most states it's easier to become a child-care worker than to get a driver's license. "Finding the best teachers enables us to put children first," Jordano continues. "We respect and develop them. We bring dignity to their work, a real challenge in a service business. Teachers in our society are undervalued when compared with doctors, lawyers, and other professionals. And the younger the child you serve, the less esteemed you are. Child care in general lacks recognition as a significant vocation.

"We pay our staff 30 to 50 percent higher than industry averages. They are full-time employees with full benefits. Our least paid teacher right out of school makes $28,000. Our competitors pay $14,000 to $16,000. How does anybody live on that? We are attracting and keeping the best people. Our turnover rate is consistently lower than the industry rate, which hovers around 45 percent."

Rosemary's care for her staff goes beyond salaries. "At the heart of what we do as an organization is our investment in the inner landscape of our teachers. Their dignity, their identity, is first and foremost. A commitment to their inner well-being translates into excellence in how they nurture and teach children.

"We recognize that good isn't good enough for children. We have to be outstanding, and being outstanding comes not just from professional competencies; it comes from the way we practice qualities like patience, tolerance, commitment, optimism, and perseverance. These qualities are commonly known as virtues, though the V-word isn't used much in business. Work is a manifestation, not only of our professional interest but also of our personal values. The *way* we do our work is as important as *what* we do."

Enrich the Communities Where You Do Business

Jordano believes business is an efficient and powerful vehicle for social change, and she is committed to helping the children and families in the communities where ChildrenFirst operates. ChildrenFirst has donated their teachers as volunteers in emerging literacy programs. They also teach seminars on parenting and give training in CPR, first aid, and child development. Parents may use the extensive library of materials at each ChildrenFirst center.

ChildrenFirst has also participated in such ventures as America's Promise Summit on Volunteerism, led by General Colin Powell, and City Year in Boston. In New York, Boston, and Chicago they have worked with Reach Out and Read programs.

ChildrenFirst invites nonprofit organizations serving children and families to use their centers. They also provide backup child care for the volunteers and staff of these agencies, including Jumpstart and the Wildcat Service Corporation, a welfare-to-work initiative in New York City.

Speaking of New York, in September 1999, then First Lady Hillary Rodham Clinton visited the grand reopening of ChildrenFirst at Rockefeller Center and spoke about the importance of backup child care. "ChildrenFirst is really on the cutting edge of how we are going to deal with those productivity, economic, loyalty, and other issues raised by child care in the workplace," she said. "Very few parents are fortunate enough to have the kind of facility and the well-trained staff that is available here at ChildrenFirst."

"Education in general, and child care in particular, have never been lucrative," says Jordano. "People who are drawn to this work have a disposition that is motivated more by serving others than by money. For me, serving gives my life meaning and grows out of my relationship with God and my belief that this is how he intends life to be used."

SAFE AND SOUND

Deploy a Safety Net between You and the Ground

Some people thrive on the danger of working without a net, but most entrepreneurs draw courage from knowing there is something between them and the ground. For Rosemary, that safety net is her family.

"Starting and growing a business means having an incredible tolerance for ambiguity," she says. "Having a strong family behind me lessens my fear of taking risks. When the first round of investors came to our board meeting, my dad sat in with us. It was so wonderful to have him there in the room. I found out the next night that his brother had died two days earlier. Instead of going to the funeral, he came to the board meeting. When I asked him about it he said, 'I have a daughter who is trying to change the world and I love her very much. I loved my brother too. There was nothing I could do for him at the funeral, but I could make a difference by being here with you.' It's that kind of support that allows me to give so much to my vision.

"Many of my good habits come from my dad. He goes to church every morning. We get to spend time together when I can join him, and afterwards we get a cup of coffee and he walks me home. I enjoy attending daily mass with him when I'm in town. People ask me how I find the time when I'm so busy running a company. My response is, 'I can run a company *because* I fit it in.'

"I structure my life to include church and prayer because they make it much easier to do what I need to do when I get to the office. Prayer and reflection are necessary components of a meaningful life. They are hard to do with all the craziness business brings, but they make you a more effective person, and this, in turn, benefits your whole organization."

Leave an Indelible Impact on Those You Serve

In *The Moral Intelligence of Children*, Robert Coles writes, "The child is a witness; the child is an ever-attentive witness of grown-up morality—or lack thereof; the child looks for cues as to how one ought to behave and finds them galore as we parents and teachers go about our lives, making choices, addressing people, showing in action our rock-bottom assumptions, desires, and values, and thereby telling those young observers much more than they realize."[8]

Can a child-care company offering temporary care make a permanent impression on these inscrutable enigmas? ChildrenFirst believes so. Their latest annual report notes, "Each moment of a child's life, especially small children, is an intensive, concentrated instance when important developmental seeds are sown . . . . Fyodor Dostoyevsky wrote, in

The Brothers Karamazov, 'You must know that there is nothing higher or stronger or sounder or more useful afterwards in life than some good memory, especially a memory from childhood . . . even if one good memory remains with us in our hearts, that alone may serve some day for salvation.'"

Creating good memories is the essence of what ChildrenFirst does. Even with the intermittent nature of their care, they are having a permanent effect on the families they serve. For Rosemary Jordano, ChildrenFirst is more than her company's name—it's her life's mantra. "I hope one day to have my own family," she concludes, "and to be experiencing all this with my own children."

When that happens, she will be well rehearsed for the role.

SUMMARY OF KEY PRINCIPLES

- Use your head to follow your heart.
- Find a way around roadblocks.
- Pull the trigger when passion and profit line up.
- Prepare your supply lines in advance.
- Document the need for your services.
- Specialize in win-win solutions.
- Set the standard for excellence in your field.
- Enrich the communities where you do business.
- Deploy a safety net between you and the ground.
- Leave an indelible impact on those you serve.

INFLUENTIAL BOOKS— RECOMMENDED READING

Coles, Robert. *The Spiritual Life of Children.* Boston: Houghton Mifflin, 1990.

Collins, James C., and Jerry I. Porras. *Built to Last: Successful Habits of Visionary Companies.* New York: HarperBusiness, 1994.

Frankl, Viktor. *Man's Search for Meaning.* New York: Washington Square Press, 1959.

Sendak, Maurice. *Where the Wild Things Are.* New York: HarperCollins, 1988.

Stegner, Wallace. *Crossing to Safety.* New York: Penguin, 1987.

JAMES H. AMOS JR., is president and CEO of Mail Boxes Etc. (MBE), the world's largest and fastest-growing franchiser of retail business, communication, and postal service centers. Born and raised in St. Louis, Jim attended the University of Missouri. He went through the Platoon Leaders Class Program while in college and graduated as a Marine Corps second lieutenant.

Amos then pulled two combat tours in Vietnam, where he earned twelve decorations, including the Purple Heart and the Vietnamese Cross of Gallantry. He left the Corps after eight years of service and began a business career in the franchising industry.

In 1998, the University of Missouri honored him as a scholar-in-residence. Jim is the author of two books, *The Memorial* and *Focus or Failure: America at the Crossroads*. He has been recognized in *Who's Who in American Executives* and the *International Authors and Writers Who's Who*. He is vice chairman of the International Franchise Association and serves on several other boards, including those of Mail Boxes Etc., "We Deliver Dreams" Children's Foundation, the San Diego Opera, and the University of Missouri Advisory Board.

Jim enjoys handball, playing the saxophone and reading, reading, reading. Together with his wife, Micki, and daughters, Holly and Heather, he makes his home in San Diego, California.

Chapter 10

FRANCHISING YOUR FUTURE

"The true product of a business is not what it sells but how it sells it. The true product of a business is the business itself."

MICHAEL GERBER[1]

Entrepreneur magazine ranked Mail Boxes Etc. (MBE) number seven on its 2000 list of the Top 500 Franchises and number one in the business service category, a position MBE has held for a decade. Jim Amos, the company's CEO since 1996, has been instrumental in developing the mission, vision, and core values that have enabled this stratospheric success.

MBE opened its first franchise in Carlsbad (San Diego County), California in 1980. Ten years later it had one thousand franchise locations and quickly expanded to twice that number by 1993. Today the MBE Network boasts more than four thousand independently owned centers worldwide. The company went public in 1986 and was acquired by U.S. Office Products in 1997.

On average, one new MBE location opens every business day somewhere on the globe, making MBE one of the world's fastest-growing franchise companies. By the end of 2000, MBE anticipates having more than five thousand locations operating in over sixty countries.

Entrepreneur: James H. Amos Jr.
Company: Mail Boxes Etc.
**   San Diego, California**
Year Started: 1980
Start-up Costs: $140,000
1999 Revenues: $1,500,000,000
Employees: 12,200 (system-wide)

BIG BUSINESS

Commit to a Concept with a Future

"I resigned my commission in the Marines in 1973," Jim Amos recalls, "and a friend and I started a career counseling business called Pierson Associates. The company grew until Bernard Haldane & Associates—at that time the largest career counseling company in the world—bought us. After the sale I went to work for Arby's in their franchising division for several years. Insty Prints recruited me from Arby's, and from there I moved to the Brice Group in Dallas, where I served as president and CEO for nine years until we sold the company. Then came MBE."

The common thread in the colorful tapestry of Jim's career is franchising. "Most people don't realize that franchising is such a powerful economic engine," he says. "It generates about a trillion dollars in sales in the United States—about half of every retail dollar spent—and employs more than eight million people. There are about fifteen hundred franchisers in over seventy industries that account for 600,000 stores and centers of all stripes. Every eight minutes a new franchise opens its doors and these new businesses create 170,000 new jobs a year.

"Franchising works from mom-and-pop businesses to mega franchisees, a growing trend in the world of franchising. Multiple store owners comprise about 31 percent of our system."

Don't Reinvent the Wheel

Franchising began more than one hundred years ago with Singer Sewing Machines. The earliest franchises were trade-name franchises like Coca-Cola or General Motors, where trade names and products were transferred to an authorized reseller. In 1952 Ray Kroc bought out the McDonald brothers and pioneered what's now known as Business Format Franchising. In his book *The E-Myth Revisited,* Michael Gerber defines a Business Format Franchise as "a proprietary way of doing business that successfully and preferentially differentiates every extraordinary business from every one of its competitors."[2]

"In Business Format Franchising," Amos adds, "you transfer not just the trade name and product, but you also provide the entrepreneur with a complete operational system. There hasn't been a more significant economic development in the world since franchising took on this form. With Business Format Franchising you don't have to reinvent the wheel. As an entrepreneur, you step into an established way of doing business with proven economic viability. You essentially take the hand of the franchisee and walk them through a process that's already proven successful in the marketplace.

"This is usually a safer course than risking your own capital on an unproven business," Jim continues. "Success is never guaranteed, but every franchisee has a guaranteed opportunity to succeed to whatever level they choose depending on how much time and energy they want to invest in their business."

BEST BUY

Lower Your Risk with a Business Format Franchise

Michael Gerber has the numbers to back up the claim that franchising is the safest way to do business. "Businesses start and fail in the United States at an increasingly staggering rate. Every year over a million people in this country start a business of some sort. Statistics tell us that by the end of the first year at least 40 percent of them will be out of business. Within five years, more than 80 percent of them—800,000—will have failed . . . [but], according to studies conducted by the U.S. Commerce Department from 1971 to 1987, less than 5 percent of franchises have been terminated on an annual basis, or 25 percent in five years. Compare that statistic to the more than 80 percent failure rate of independently owned businesses, and you can immediately understand the power of the Turn-Key Revolution in our economy."[3]

Amos, the incoming chairman of the International Franchise Association, points out, "Next to securities, Business Format Franchising is the most regulated business in the U.S. There are thirty-one regulatory agencies that determine how a single franchise is sold. Franchisers are required by federal law to file a Uniform Franchise Offering Circular that has twenty-three specific disclosures in it. A potential franchisee must sign a receipt upon receiving these disclosures and wait ten days before doing a transaction with a franchiser."

Raise Your Chance of Success by Getting Branded

Cashing in on the charisma of a name brand is another benefit of franchising. "The power of branding is exponential," Amos asserts, "because you have something much more attractive to a wider base of potential customers than you have with a nonbranded item. Let's say I open a hamburger shop and I am successful. I'm doing a million dollars in annual sales, the same as the other hamburger restaurant across the street. Now, my sign says 'Joe's Hamburgers,' and the other sign reads 'McDonalds.' The cash flow may be the same, but which business has more liquidity value? The branded store will sell for a lot more than an independent store.

"Then there's the operational and marketing support you get with a branded product. National marketing campaigns are a good example. We've had commercial spots during the last several Super Bowls. This level of exposure is tremendously beneficial and brings a great deal of credibility to the franchise owner.

"When considering franchise opportunities," Amos cautions, "it's smart to look at a franchise that's been around and has proven successful in the marketplace. I always encourage a potential franchisee to talk to existing franchisees. Ask them how they like the franchise, and find out what kind of relationship they have with the franchiser."

BETWEEN FRIENDS

Concentrate on Maintaining Good Relationships

This last point is critical according to Amos. "Franchising is the most synergistic business in the world because it's so relationship driven. That's why I love it. We have a vice president of franchise relations who does nothing but interface with franchisees. Everything depends on the goodwill between the franchiser and franchisee. The franchiser becomes an enabling agent to help people realize their dreams. In fact, that's why at MBE we say, 'We deliver dreams.'"

Good relationships depend on mutual trust and moral character. "As an employer and franchiser I look for people who have good character first, then competence in their discipline," says this ex-Marine. "If you have the most competent person in the world yet have no character, you are untrustworthy.

Or, if you have the highest level of character and integrity yet are incompetent, you are still untrustworthy. These two must be in balance. Still, I always give the nod to character because you can train and teach the skill. It's much more difficult to instill character and integrity into someone."

Instill Moral Values into Your Business

"Every time I've had the opportunity to instill moral values into a business entity, the results have been astounding," says the CEO of MBE. "When values and beliefs become embodied in the workplace, they intensify employees' commitment, enthusiasm, and drive. Once they are embedded in the warp and woof of a business, communication improves. Values lift the integrity of management's decision making and a manager's ability to evaluate personnel and projects.

"One of the first things I did after taking the helm of Mail Boxes Etc. was to bring in Sister Suzanne Donovan, a Catholic nun who also happens to be a clinical psychologist and holds an MBA, to lead our entire company in determining our values. I have worked with Suzanne for over ten years in strategic planning. Every associate, board member, selected members of our franchise family and vendor community participated. The values we identified over a week's time were caring, honesty, fairness, integrity, trust, respect, commitment, and accountability. It's my opinion that in today's business world, you should be willing to experiment with and change anything at any time with the single exception of values; they are inviolate."[4]

"Core values are the organization's essential and enduring tenets—a small set of timeless guiding principles that require no external justification," write Jim Collins and Jerry Porras in *Built to Last*. "They have intrinsic value and importance to those inside the organization . . . . The key point is that an enduring great company decides for itself what values it holds to be core, largely independent of the current environment, competitive requirements, or management fads."[5]

Team Up with Trusted Partners to Offer Better Services

While old-fashioned values are foundational to the way MBE does business, the company and its CEO are just as committed to newfangled ideas. MBE lives out its motto, "Making Business Easier Worldwide," by making state-of-the-art technology accessible and affordable not only to its franchisees but also to general consumers and the small office/home office (SOHO) market.

MBE does this through strategic partnerships with industry and technology leaders. A few examples: MBE works with Hughes Network Systems to link satellite technology with point-of-sale computer systems in participating centers. This satellite technology allows high-speed communications and Internet connectivity for network operations.

In April 1999 eBay, the world's leading online trading community, designated MBE as its exclusive referral shipping solution with their franchises serving as drop-off and pickup locations for e-commerce shipments. Then there's MBE Online, a collaboration with IBM and Infoseek that provides a package of online services and resources geared for small businesses. The company is also working with the U.S. Postal Service to establish MBE centers as U.S. Postal Service Authorized Retail Outlets.

Successful partnerships have to be championed from the top, and Amos appears to be doing a masterful job of creating win-win relationships based on mutual trust. "'Too many partnerships fail because they don't get the resources and credibility within the organization,'" John Chambers, CEO of Cisco Systems, tells *Wired* magazine. "'When we started to do this, I took one of my top guys and made him a senior vice president for strategic partnerships. He reports directly to me and has his own staff, so he doesn't have to go begging for the help he needs.' His (Chamber's) dream date: Hewlett-Packard. 'HP has created a culture where their word is their bond. We have dozens of alliances going on with that company, and not a single contract. That's my kind of partner.'"[6]

BETTER WAY

Practice Forgiveness as a Way of Life

Amos believes in order to stay in positive relationships with people one has to practice forgiveness as a way of life. Forgiveness isn't often found on the list of characteristics of a good CEO, but Jim says it belongs near the top.

"Some may think it's a weakness to be willing to forgive. I'm more afraid of *not* forgiving, because I understand the Scriptures to teach that

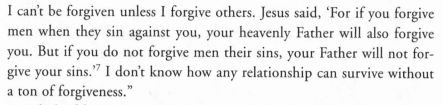

I can't be forgiven unless I forgive others. Jesus said, 'For if you forgive men when they sin against you, your heavenly Father will also forgive you. But if you do not forgive men their sins, your Father will not forgive your sins.'[7] I don't know how any relationship can survive without a ton of forgiveness."

A lack of forgiveness not only creates relational problems; it can also be expensive. "We have become a litigious society because of our inability to love and forgive," Amos writes in *Focus or Failure*. "I have had the good fortune to travel the world many times over as the chief executive officer of multinational companies. I have found most of the world stands with mouth agape at the size of American legal documents and the lack of trust they demonstrate. In Japan, as an example, most business agreements are done with only a handshake. Furthermore, only 6 percent of all of their disagreements are ever litigated. Unfortunately, as the Japanese have had to deal more and more with America, their legal documents become larger and larger.

"I know there are hard-nosed business men and women reading these words laughing to themselves, knowing that 'you must cover your rear' with legal documents to succeed. I do not disagree. But how sad! I have been thrilled, however, to make friends around the world. And I will tell you that while our companies also don the armor of our legal documents, every relationship we have developed in expanding internationally has been built on trust. Our growth has not been driven by written agreements but by mutual willingness to live up to the unwritten elements of each agreement. What are these unwritten elements? Mutual respect, trust, the right attitude, effective leadership, and—yes—even love and forgiveness."[8]

To personally forgive an employee or manager for unethical behavior or a bad decision doesn't mean you ignore their actions. "Forgiveness and accountability are two completely different things in business," Amos clarifies. "There are consequences to be faced and dealt with. I recently had to fire a person who has been with me for ten years, not because of ethical or moral issues, but because the company had simply passed him by. But the relationship, the commitment to friendship hasn't gone away. Our friendship will survive."

See Yourself as Working for Your Father's Company

Jim smiles when he says, "I look at what I'm doing as if I'm working for my father's company. When you're working for your dad, you see things differently.

"I didn't grow up in a Christian home, but after I left for college, my parents became very active in the church and have been ever since. As a young lad I used to go to a summer Bible school at a small Presbyterian church, and the teaching impacted my life. But not until Vietnam did I come face-to-face with mortality and realize the truth of the old saying, 'There are no atheists in foxholes.'

"I reached a point in 1973, while wrestling with the decision to leave the Marines, that I bowed my head at my desk one day and asked the Lord Jesus into my life. That's when I began this journey, this lifelong process of learning to live by God's principles and values. It's hard to understand how I used to live or how other folks live without a relationship with the Lord."

Jim's openness about his faith has had repercussions. "There are always those who take exception to the public nature of my faith," he acknowledges, "but for me, it's who I am. I can't separate Sunday from the rest of the week, nor do I believe I should. However, I think there's a certain degree of sensitivity that goes together with walking the talk.

"I know I'm where I am because of the Lord. I have no delusions about that. It's not talent or ability. I'm here because God allows me to be here. I have a sense of destiny about what I'm doing at MBE that causes me to pray my way through every day. I'm well aware that on my own I don't have the wisdom, understanding, or knowledge necessary to lead or carry the responsibilities I have. I need and depend on my Lord and Savior.

"I don't know how people survive without him. I certainly couldn't."

SUMMARY OF KEY PRINCIPLES

- Commit to a concept with a future.
- Don't reinvent the wheel.
- Lower your risk with a Business Format Franchise.
- Raise your chance of success by getting branded.
- Concentrate on maintaining good relationships.
- Instill moral values into your business.

- Team up with trusted partners to offer better services.
- Practice forgiveness as a way of life.
- See yourself as working for your father's company.

INFLUENTIAL BOOKS— RECOMMENDED READING

Bunyan, John. *Pilgrim's Progress.* Nelson's Royal Classics Series. Nashville: Thomas Nelson, 1999.

Drucker, Peter F. *Managing for Results: Economic Tasks and Risk-Taking Decisions.* New York: HarperBusiness, 1993.

Gerber, Michael F. *The E-Myth Revisited: Why Most Small Businesses Don't Work and What to Do About It.* New York: HarperBusiness, 1995.

Greenleaf, Robert K. *On Becoming a Servant Leader.* San Francisco: Jossey-Bass, 1996.

JEFFREY MCKEEVER has received many honors, including being named Master Entrepreneur of the Year by *Inc.* magazine (1995) and Arizona Entrepreneur of the Year by Arizona State University (1984). In 1997 he became one of the youngest men ever to be inducted into the Arizona Business Hall of Fame.

The greatest honor may be his induction into the computer industry Hall of Fame at Comdex '97. The fourteen other charter members include computer greats Bill Gates, Andy Grove, and Steve Jobs. In 1998 McKeever was named one of the computer industry's Top 25 Executives for the thirteenth consecutive year by *Computer Reseller News*.

Jeffrey logged on in Marion, Indiana, and grew up in Tucson, Arizona. In 1965 he received a B.S. with a major in accounting from the University of Arizona and then joined the Air Force, having graduated at the top of his ROTC class. When his eyesight prevented him from becoming a pilot, he got involved in computers and ran a computer center in Japan. Following his military stint, he returned to the University of Arizona for his M.B.A.

McKeever eventually got his pilot's license. He loves to fly and continues to get new ratings, which, he says, is why he's not very good at golf. His other lifelong passion is photography. He makes his home in Paradise Valley, Arizona, together with his wife, Tahnia, and daughter. He has a grown son by a previous marriage.

Chapter 11

VIRTUAL REALITY

"The Future is in Beta."
WIRED MAGAZINE[1]

MicroAge, Inc. is the largest company in this book, posting FY '97 revenues of $4.5 billion, an increase of 23 percent over FY '96. Not surprisingly, it's a computer company.

One of its greatest achievements according to cofounder Jeff McKeever is survival. In 1999 the company morphed into two Fortune 500 companies, MicroAge Technology Services and Pinacor. "I think [McKeever is] one of the best long-term thinkers in the business," says Robert Anastasi, managing director of the Robinson-Humphrey Co. "They've reinvented the company a couple of times, and he's been able to drive the change."

ABORT, RETRY, IGNORE

Turn Disappointments into Discoveries

McKeever got his start in business when he won an instamatic camera at the grand opening of a photography store. He fell in love with photography and opened his own studio at age fourteen.

"My father was a creative person," recalls McKeever, "but being a commercial artist, he didn't have much money. In my early twenties I somewhat resented that my parents couldn't do much for me. Yet by the time I reached my thirties, I was thankful they couldn't because what they did

Entrepreneur: Jeff McKeever
Company: MicroAge, Inc.
Tempe, Arizona
Year Started: 1976
Start-up Costs: $30,000
1997 Revenues: $4,500,000,000
Employees: 5,000

give me proved much more important—a chance to become self-reliant. The things no one can take from me include the values I learned from my parents and the church I grew up in.

"I had a photography studio while in high school and I continued that into college. I got into the Air Force ROTC, but I didn't pass the vision test after graduation so I couldn't become a pilot. This hit me as a major disappointment. I had the option of selecting another field, and I picked computers, which turned out to be a good choice.

"When you meet with disappointments," Jeff says, "you need to rethink them. Things that don't go your way are sometimes signals for bigger opportunities if you're open to that possibility. I'm reminded of the story of a religious man who, in a flood, climbs to his rooftop. Soon a rowboat comes along and offers to rescue him, but he says, 'No, I believe God will protect and deliver me.' Another rowboat comes by in a bit and the same thing happens. Now the water reaches his knees and a helicopter tries to rescue him. He says, 'No, I believe in God and I'll be fine.' Next thing you know he's at the pearly gates. 'I don't understand,' he complains to God. 'I trusted you and you let me down.' God replies, 'I don't know what more I could have done—I sent you two rowboats and a helicopter.'

"As an entrepreneur you need an openness to what comes your way. Things may not be what you expect; yet that doesn't mean they won't prove better than what you planned."

Act Today on What You Expect to Happen Tomorrow

"After five years on active duty," McKeever continues, "I came back to Tucson and went to work for a bank to pay my way through graduate school. I had a wife and child, so I viewed the job initially as just a way to make ends meet. But whatever I do, I always work hard at it. Soon I became a VP and an understudy of the bank's president. When the bank merged with First National Bank of Arizona, I accepted a transfer to Phoenix.

"One of the people working for me there was Alan Hald, a charismatic Harvard Business School grad with a high IQ. Alan was involved with the World Future Society, and we started talking about the future at lunch one day. He mentioned how the increased pace of technology since World War II was changing our society. A second dynamic was the seventy-seven million

Americans born between 1946 and 1964—the baby boomers—and their impact as a group. Then there was the progress being made in microelectronics, fueled by the invention of integrated circuits and microprocessors."

In 1975 computers were a nascent industry. Personal PCs lay just over the horizon, but Hald saw the world on the verge of a new renaissance. "This renaissance would rely heavily on the personal use of computers, which would enable many people to communicate simultaneously," Hald believed. "I said to Jeff, 'This is the beginning of the new economy. A colossal, unmet need is about to be recognized, and if we're going to start a business, this is where to do it.'"[2]

"I didn't need a lot of coaching to understand the implications of the microcomputer," Jeff recalls. "We discussed leaving the bank and opening a store to sell these new computer kits."

GOING DIGITAL

Mortgage the Present to Build the Future

The dynamic duo put second mortgages on their homes, refinanced their cars, and used numerous credit cards to raise $15,000 each. While financial planners will blanch at this point, McKeever and Hald aren't unique in launching a successful business on a raft of credit cards. Jim Liemandt started Trinity Development Group by maxing out thirty-five cards. (Trinity's 1996 revenues topped $120 million.)[3]

Tom Peters points out that according to "*Inc.* magazine's list of 500 top-growth companies: 34 percent of the Inc. 500 were launched with less than $10,000; 59 percent with less than $50,000; and 75 percent with less than $100,000. We may be in an age of great sophistication, but a handful of dollars, mostly garnered by putting a second mortgage on the house and shaking down Aunt Sally, will still allow you to get into most any business you can name."[4]

Consider these other low-budget computer start-ups: Ross Perot began EDS in 1962 with $1,000 and by 1997 had revenues of $14.4 billion. Apple Computer, founded by Steve Jobs and Steve Wozniak in 1976 with $1,350, had 1997 revenues of $7.1 billion. Dell Computer, launched in 1984 by Michael Dell for $1,000, generated $11 billion in 1997 revenues.[5]

With their hip-pocket capital, Jeff and Alan formed the Phoenix Group, Inc. A coin toss made McKeever the chairman and Hald the president. They contacted Paul Terrell, owner of Byte Shop, Inc., and secured the rights to use the name in Arizona. Details of the agreement were written on a dinner napkin and then signed. (Later, the name MicroAge—an integration of the *micro*computer with the information *age*—was chosen over lunch at a local restaurant.)

Jeff and Alan quit their bank jobs and, in September 1976, opened the first computer store in Arizona—and one of the first in the nation. "We started out selling technology that wasn't even market tested or market ready," remembers McKeever. "As a matter of fact, Steve Jobs was still in his garage tinkering with his apples when we started."

With limited cash the partners kept little stock on hand. They took prepaid orders, then got the product by mail, keeping overhead and risk relatively low. By the end of November, sales topped $40,000 and they decided to open another Byte Shop in Phoenix.

Beware of Means That Blur the End

"The Byte Shop did $1.5 million in revenue our first year," notes Jeff, "$8 million our second, and $15 million our third year. We make more money than that in a day now. We continued adding locations, and by 1980 we had a $30 million company. We had become the largest entrepreneurial company in the industry with the exception of Apple. We became the nation's largest wholesale distributor, but we recognized this wouldn't be enough and decided to get into the franchise business.

"We had a vision that the microcomputer would revolutionize the world," Jeff goes on to say. "But we got this notion of franchising and became so enthralled with it that we lost sight of our broader mission. It's easy in any business to get infatuated with some new element and lose sight of the bigger picture. We got fixated on franchising and lost our focus. That's how I felt by the mid-1980s, after successfully turning the company around. I came to a different view in the early 1990s. I realized that if it weren't for franchising we might not have survived. It may have taken us into Chapter 11 earlier than we might have otherwise gone, but none of the other wholesale distributors from the 1970s survived. We made it because franchising gave us something of interest to a venture capitalist—Olivetti—which decided to invest $5 million in us precisely because of our franchising."

TROUBLESHOOTING

Redefine Yourself around a Stable Core

The company emerged from Chapter 11 in October 1982, grew to $142 million by 1985, and completed an initial public offering in 1987. "In 1988 through 1990, we redefined the company and focused it specifically on franchise business," McKeever says. "We became the most successful franchiser in the U.S. by 1989, only to realize this wasn't the world of the future."

MicroAge evolved from a retailer into the largest distributor in its industry, then went on to become the most successful franchiser. Their current emphasis is on systems integration and strategic partnerships with other major players. "Our future at MicroAge will be more tied to services and less tied to product," McKeever says in *The MicroAge Way*. "If you don't add value, you're getting squeezed out of the equation. If a dealer is not becoming a value-added reseller (VAR) or system integrator, he is in the business of going out of business."[6]

"We are in a business of change and chaos," continues McKeever. "Our strategies and tactics change all the time, but our values remain constant. They are important to us. You'll see them in all our buildings. Most associates carry the MicroAge Value Card, which has on it our mission, our quality statement, and our six core values: Add value to everything we do; respect our relationships; act with integrity; make things happen; do it right the first time; have fun."

Lead from Your Values

This commitment to a set of values has remained constant through all the structural changes at MicroAge. "I grew up in a very strong Christian home," Jeff says, "and went to church about three times a week as a kid. My family and I are still very active in the Presbyterian church, and the values I learned there have shaped my life. When Alan and I started MicroAge, we had a much broader vision than just making money. We wanted to be a part of changing the way the world works. Very early on we knew we wanted to manage based on values.

"CEOs have to make a lot of tough calls," McKeever says knowingly. "A business enterprise is all about making decisions and trade-offs. If you have a values-based thought process, you will make better decisions."

McKeever is right. In his research for a forthcoming book, Frank Toney demonstrates that "business leaders who 'always' apply the teachings of their religion attain superior goal achievement results in nearly every category over those who 'never' apply the teachings of their religion. The companies they govern earn an average of 8 percent more profit. There are corresponding greater annual increases in their personal worth. Their personal lives also benefit from an average 6 percent stronger feelings of fulfillment and satisfaction. On the average, they are healthier, live longer and give over twice as much to community and charitable causes."[7]

Leading from moral values may pay dividends, but it can also be expensive. "In coming out of Chapter 11," Jeff recounts, "we could have easily done a cram-down—get everyone to take a bit of a haircut. But instead, over a five-year period, we paid every one of our creditors back with interest (a 6 percent dividend in cash and preferred stock). That wasn't the best business decision, but it was the right moral decision."

Maintain the Tension between Control and Growth

According to this accountant-turned-CEO, "One of our greatest challenges is managing the tension between control and growth. Growing a business at 30 to 40 percent annually for twenty-plus years and maintaining control at the same time is tricky.

"It's like walking a tightrope: if you lean too far either way you get in trouble. If the accountant in me comes out strongly and I put too much emphasis on the control side, I can definitely stop the growth. I've done it for brief periods when necessary. You have to know when it's necessary. On the other hand, when you start pushing your people for growth, you can get it, but the price is always decreased control.

"Your people determine your ability to successfully hand over control. We've been blessed in being able to attract and retain great executives. If you want executives who can exert strong leadership, you must give them the opportunity to fail. If you don't let people fail, you can't build. You don't go from $30,000 to $4.5 billion without taking risks. You don't get there without inducing others to join you in the vision and giving them enough freedom to take risks on their own, accepting the consequences that they will fail from time to time."

McKeever goes on to say, "I'm determined to look for the good in people. A leader should help people see what's right about themselves and feel good about who they are and what they can do. Attacking people demoralizes them and robs them of their sense of self-worth. And this ultimately robs the company."

Service What You Sell

"You will never again have a competitive advantage on product or price," says Don Beveridge, "service is the only advantage."[8] From the beginning MicroAge put a premium on service. The MicroAge Promise guaranteed a MicroAge computer system would operate trouble-free for a year, or it would be repaired or replaced without inconvenience to the customer.

In 1991 MicroAge created the Quality Integration Center, which could configure twenty thousand units per month. In 1994 MicroAge became one of the first companies in their field awarded ISO certification, the highest international quality standard for integration services. All the efforts paid off. *Computerworld* magazine recognized them as the top systems integrator in 1997.

GUI

Take Care of All Your Stakeholders

"Our stockholders are people who have expectations about our company," says the man responsible for results at MicroAge. "We have an obligation to produce profits for them. We have to keep our promises because of what this means to their lives and to their retirement plans. But we also have a responsibility to do what's right by all our stakeholders, including associates, suppliers, and customers.

So what happens when producing profits for stockholders means laying off associates? According to McKeever, "When this happens, we provide a good severance package. I'm a member of the same community as many of the associates. I'm going to run into them again. Some time ago I attended a function at my daughter's school and saw a woman we had laid off two years earlier. She was a good associate, let go simply because we no longer needed her skills. Because of her tenure, she had received six months' severance pay.

"I wondered how she would react to me. She came over right away, smiled, and shook my hand. She explained that, thanks to the severance package, she was able to stay home for a few months with her two small children. Soon she and her husband found a way to restructure their lives so she could be a stay-at-home mom, and she thanked me.

"I have a theory about life, and it applies to me as an employer. The associates at MicroAge only want to know one thing about me. Do I care about them as people? The fact that I do makes all the difference. In business you have many opportunities to interact with people. It's easy to engage with them only in terms of what they're supposed to do, but I try to remind myself to look at people as children of God and not as instruments to achieve goals. Seeing people this way affects how I treat them."

Be Unreasonable about Progress

In *Man and Superman*, George Bernard Shaw wrote, "The reasonable man adapts himself to the world, the unreasonable one persists in trying to adapt the world to himself. Therefore, all progress depends on unreasonable men."

McKeever and Hald are among the most unreasonable men of the twentieth century. What they accomplished played an important role in "the beginning of creating the true physical information infrastructure of the world. Everything else is now built on top of that," Hald mused in a 1996 interview. "The Internet is successful because there are so many PCs out there. So, we were the revolutionaries that helped build, and still are building, the physical layer of the Information Age."[9]

"The Internet is the next wave," Jeff echoes. "Tremendous opportunities await entrepreneurs on the net. At MicroAge we've spent the last twenty years helping build the infrastructure, which for others is just now becoming real."

McKeever hasn't made any plans beyond MicroAge. He doesn't need to make more money, but he still wants to make a difference. "Making money is inconsequential ultimately," says Jeff. "You like to make it because it gives you the resources with which you can project your values in a broader way in life, but it's not the most important thing." Or, as Sinbad quips, "Always remember, it's only money—they print more of it every day."[10]

"I get up early every morning," McKeever says thoughtfully, "usually by 3:30 A.M. I like to spend time in the early morning thinking about my relationship with God and my place in the world. In some ways we are very insignificant, and yet one person can make a difference. We are God's children, and he can give us tremendous power to do the right thing. I still see tremendous opportunities to change the way the world works through MicroAge. As long as that's possible, I want to be part of it."

SUMMARY OF KEY PRINCIPLES
- Turn disappointments into discoveries.
- Act today on what you expect to happen tomorrow.
- Mortgage the present to build the future.
- Beware of means that blur the end.
- Redefine yourself around a stable core.
- Lead from your values.
- Maintain the tension between control and growth.
- Service what you sell.
- Take care of *all* your stakeholders.
- Be unreasonable about progress.

INFLUENTIAL BOOKS— RECOMMENDED READING

David, Stan, and Cristopher Meyers. *Blur: The Speed of Change in the Connected Economy.* New York: Warner Books, 1999.

Huntington, Samuel P. *The Clash of Civilizations and the Remaking of World Order.* New York: Simon & Schuster, 1998.

Moore, James F. *The Death of Competition.* New York: HarperCollins, 1996.

Stalk, George. *Competing Against Time.* New York: Simon & Schuster, 1990.

Taylor, Jim, and Watts Wicker. *The 500 Year Delta.* New York: HarperCollins, 1997.

S. TRUETT CATHY presides over one of the fastest-growing restaurant chains in America. For more than fifty years, he's been a restaurateur with a southern gentleman's hospitality. Cathy has received dozens of awards for his business and community service. These include the 1997 New-comen Society Award (for exceptional contributors to the American free enterprise system), the 1996 Georgia Freedom Award, the 1992 National Caring Award (given to the 10 Most Caring People in the Nation by the Caring Institute in Washington, D.C.), and the 1989 Horatio Alger Award.

Truett, sneaking up on eighty, still rides his Harley and enjoys trail bikes, a passion he shares with his son, Dan. He's a trustee emeritus of Clayton State University and has been a Sunday school teacher for most of the past forty-three years at First Baptist Church in Jonesboro, Georgia, the Cathys' hometown. Truett and his wife, Jeannette, have three children and twelve grandchildren.

DAN CATHY, Truett's oldest son, is executive vice president of Chick-fil-A, Inc. and president of Chick-fil-A International. He began his career at age nine, singing for customers and doing radio spots for the restaurant.

Since graduating from Georgia Southern College with a degree in business administration, he's opened more than fifty Chick-fil-A restaurants while serving as director of operations. He has also completed the owner/president management course at Harvard Business School.

Dan's hobbies include flying and running. He has competed in both the Los Angeles and Boston Marathons. He is on the board of directors of Wachovia Bank and the board of councilors of the Carter Center. He also serves on the Foundation of Gordon College and is a member of the International Society of Business Fellows. Dan and his wife, Rhonda, have two sons and live in Fayetteville, Georgia.

DON (BUBBA) CATHY is senior vice president of Chick-fil-A, Inc. and president of Dwarf House, Inc., which operates eleven family dining locations in metro Atlanta. He is also supervising development of a new family dining concept called Truett's Grill.

Bubba joined the company in 1976 and worked in several positions before being named to his current post in 1995. He holds a B.A. in marketing from Samford University in Birmingham, Alabama. He enjoys water sports, sailing, tennis, racquetball, and spending time with his six children. His house in Jonesboro doubles as a neighborhood youth center and is a "TV-free zone." Together with his wife, Cindy, Bubba teaches the newlywed class at First Baptist Church in Jonesboro.

Chapter 12

WHEN LIFE HANDS YOU A CHICKEN, MAKE A SANDWICH

"God put within each of us the quest for success. If he had not, we would still be cooking over an open fire. So, here's to the winners, for they give each task their best effort and find in the end, it's easier to succeed than fail."

S. TRUETT CATHY[1]

While not inventing the chicken, S. Truett Cathy is credited with creating the modern chicken sandwich, which has helped him build one of the largest privately held restaurant chains in the nation with nearly nine hundred outlets.

According to the National Restaurant Association, "Only when compared to the quick-service industry as a whole is the magnitude of Chick-fil-A's performance truly recognized. Sales increases at Chick-fil-A were more than seven times the projected real growth for the quick-service industry as a whole. Chick-fil-A achieved its thirty-second year of growth. Their ongoing success cannot be traced back to any one cause, but rather to the combination of several successful programs, policies, and activities that have become an integral part of how Chick-fil-A does business."

Their 1999 sales numbers were over $946 million—an 18.4 percent increase

Entrepreneurs: S. Truett Cathy, Dan Cathy, Bubba Cathy
Company: Chick-fil-A, Inc.
Atlanta, Georgia
Year Started: 1946
Start-up Costs: $10,600
1999 Revenues: $946,129,000
Chain Employees: 40,000

over 1998. Chick-fil-A is on track to reach their goal of $1 billion in sales by 2000. That's not chicken feed.

A CHICKEN AMONG COWS

Pour a Solid Foundation of Hard Work

"When I was a kid," the senior Cathy tells Lea Davis Paul in *QSR* magazine, "I knew if I was going to have anything I would have to work for it. I got started in business at eight years old, buying six Cokes for a quarter and selling them for a nickel apiece. I sold magazines and had a paper route for seven straight years . . . . Taking care of the customer is something I learned early. For my paper route, we bought papers wholesale, sold them at retail, and provided delivery service. I saw I had to be punctual, dependable and friendly. The same principles today drive my business."[2]

In his article, "Fifty Years of Building a Good Name," Furman Bisher, columnist for the *Atlanta Journal-Constitution*, picks up the story a few years later.

When he came out of the army in 1946, Cathy decided it was time to go into business on his own. "I didn't know what it would be, a filling station or a store," he said, "but I was ready to commit myself to something." He was 25 years old when he and Ben, a younger brother, decided to open a small coffee shop in Hapeville, and the size of it dictated the name—Dwarf Grill. Ten counter stools and four tables, open 24 hours a day.

He rented a room next door so he could be on call at any time, and there were times, they say, when he worked 36-hour shifts with only a nap to reinforce his energy. "If we'd known what we were up against, we probably wouldn't have started, but once we opened, there was no way we were going to fail."[3]

Find the Right Place for Your Business Concept to Blossom

"Dad opened the first restaurant in 1946, a mom-and-pop diner featuring a short-order menu," remembers Truett's oldest son. "We—the Cathy kids—grew up filling ketchup bottles, stocking the candy counter, talking with customers, and checking out the colors of gum people would stick under the tables. Our customers consisted primarily of blue-collar workers. We sat right by the Atlanta airport and across the street from the Ford Motor assembly plant.

"Dad opened a second location in 1951. It burned to the ground, and he reopened it. When he did, he added a new item to the menu—a chicken steak sandwich, later named 'Chick-fil-A.' In 1967 we opened our first mall location in the Greenbriar Shopping Center in Atlanta. We had no idea malls were getting ready to take off like they did.

"We had a small operation with a single cash register," Dan continues. "We featured the Chick-fil-A sandwich, homemade salads, and soft drinks. Sales took off. Two years later we opened a second location in Savannah. We focused exclusively on malls during the 1970s and into the 1980s and didn't open our first restaurant outside a mall until 1986."

Insist on Superior Quality in Your Signature Products

Chick-fil-A prospers while other chains have folded. Location certainly contributes to their winning formula, but their watchword has always been quality.

"Being located in malls proved a decided advantage," Dan says. "The cost of entry is much lower as opposed to sites requiring hefty real estate and building costs. However, the real key lies in the quality of our signature products. The Chick-fil-A sandwich is highly thought of as *the* premier chicken sandwich on the market today. Originally it was unique, a chicken sandwich in the world of beef. Its uniqueness today comes from its taste."

Are the Cathys biased? Of course. But as Tom Cruise said in tribute to Muhammad Ali, "If you can do it, it isn't boasting." In the National Quality Survey conducted by Marketing and Research Counselors, Inc., the chain's core menu products have consistently ranked number one in their respective categories. The Chick-fil-A sandwich has held the number one spot thirty-two consecutive times.

"Ours is a very competitive industry," notes Bubba. "We try to make our product and service better than the competition. For instance, we fresh-squeeze our lemonade; nobody else in our industry does that. Our sandwiches are cooked in 100 percent peanut oil. Our salads and cole slaw are prepared on site daily from fresh ingredients. Most fast-food places try to engineer labor out of the food process. We try to have well-trained, competent people preparing fresh, quality food.

"Being consistent is also important," adds Truett. "A customer could eat fifty times at our restaurants, but if they have one disappointing experience, they may not come back. That's why we have to get customer service right the first time, every time."

ALL THE PEOPLE, ALL THE TIME

Strive to Satisfy Every Customer

"Our mission statement challenges us to 'Be America's best quick-service restaurant at satisfying every customer,'" says Truett. "To do that, we tell our people, 'Treat your customers like you like to be treated when you eat out.'

"That means taking care of the little things and keeping sight of what made you successful. I have to take care of individual customers. If you take care of the customer, the customer will take care of you. Never forget what causes things to happen."

Jim Barksdale, CEO of Netscape, sells bytes of a different kind, but he has the same regard for customers. "What do you think our purpose is? Making money? Selling products? Noooo! Nothing so crude as that. The purpose of this business is no more about making money than the purpose of life is to breathe . . . . Our purpose is to create and keep customers."[4]

Chick-fil-A's president and COO, James Collins, says, "Our successful marketing campaigns and new-store openings are merely a means to get more customers in the door. It's because of our restaurant operators' dedication to delivering consistently high-quality products and unsurpassed customer service that our customers continue to come back time after time."

With clear conviction, Dan states, "Lots of people in this business are financially driven as opposed to having a hospitality perspective. Hospitality is simply taking care of the needs of people. It's genuinely wanting to put out a great product and then enjoying the appreciation of your guests who love the food, the service, and the inviting environment. If you don't enjoy being around food, if you don't like being in the kitchen, if you don't like going around refilling tea and water glasses, if you don't like picking up paper off the floor, this isn't the business for you.

"Money can't be the prime motivator," he continues. "It has to be service—doing something you love for others. Yet money will come as a result of good service. We have Election Day every day in American retailing. People carry ballots in their wallets called Federal Reserve Notes. They cast them whenever they eat out. Whoever wins the most votes each day gets the privilege of staying in business to serve that customer in the future."

Be a Faithful Steward of Your People Resources

"The essence of why we're in business," emphasizes Dan, "is captured in our corporate purpose statement: 'To glorify God by being a faithful steward of what's entrusted to us and to have a positive influence on all who come in contact with Chick-fil-A. This includes our corporate staff, our operators, our team members, and the public at large.'"

Bubba speaks for the family when he says, "We believe we are stewards of all God has entrusted to us—not just of the financial resources we've accumulated, but most particularly of our people resources. One day we'll have to give an account. The Bible says 'to whom much is given, from them much will be required.' The restaurant business is labor intensive, which gives us great opportunity to make a difference in the lives of our corporate staff, our operators, and the forty thousand people affiliated with Chick-fil-A restaurants. We want to help them reach their potential.

"This is one of the reasons we emphasize educational training and leadership development," adds Dan. Chick-fil-A makes leadership scholarships available to all employees to the school of their choice. The tab for this program over the last twenty-six years has been more than $15 million.

"I teach a one-day vision-and-values course for new staff and operators," says Dan. "Afterwards I have everyone to my house for dinner. I want them to get to know my family on a personal level. I make every effort to be open and transparent and to break down barriers to relationships.

"To live out our corporate purpose we must be sharp mentally, physically, emotionally, and spiritually. We talk about maintaining balance in personal relationships, being better spouses and parents. We won't be as successful in our professional lives as God intends if we aren't successful in our personal lives."

Like son, like father. "I believe if an operator doesn't take responsibility for his family and he loses them," says Truett, "he's not going to make money. We can't expect him to do his best at work if he's got problems at home. We try to emphasize that our operators need to spend time with their families. That's one reason we're closed on Sunday—that's when operators can give themselves wholly to their families."

Reward Good Management

Chick-fil-A has one of the lowest management turnover rates in the quick-service food business, averaging 6 percent for its operators while industry figures run 35 percent and higher. Many operators have been with the company over twenty years.

"We enjoy a wonderful relationship with our operators," remarks Dan, "as evidenced by the lack of bickering and lawsuits. Although we put up the capital, we split the net profits of their restaurants with them fifty-fifty. This joins us at the hip."

This relationship with its operators is a Chick-fil-A distinctive and the main catalyst fueling their growth. "Each of our units is company owned but independently run under an operating agreement with self-employed business people," Truett explains. "Unlike a typical franchise arrangement where an independent restaurateur puts up money to open a franchise, we select individuals based on their leadership and managerial skills, not on their financial statements.

"Focusing on managerial talent," adds Dan, "instead of their checkbook enables us to tap into a tremendous pool of people who want their own businesses but don't have $500,000 to invest in a typical fast-food franchise. After completing our training program and signing an operating agreement, they give us a commitment check for $5,000. This amount hasn't changed since 1967. It's like a security deposit and is refundable if they ever leave (provided their books are in order). As part of the sublease agreement, operators are assured a base income of $30,000. After paying 15 percent of gross sales for operating expenses, they receive 50 percent of net profits from their restaurants. The average operator income runs about $82,000 a year."

HURRICANE SEASON
Preserve the Core; Push the Edge

Chick-fil-A's business approach reminds one of a hurricane. The core menu remains stable but everything else around this center moves in hundred-mile-an-hour gusts. Expansion continues unabated at home and abroad. In addition to mall eateries, there are now free-standing units, drive-thru-only outlets, Dwarf House full-service restaurants, and licensed outlets in hospitals, airports, businesses, and on college campuses.

Raising consumer awareness is a corporate passion. In the past three years Chick-fil-A launched a national marketing campaign featuring the Chick-fil-A Cows, opened the first in a line of redesigned restaurants, entered cyberspace with the debut of www.chick-fil-a.com, and became the title sponsor of the Chick-fil-A Charity Championship (LPGA) hosted by Nancy Lopez and the Chick-fil-A Peach Bowl, which in 1999 set a new attendance record.

"The Bible is a great business tool," remarks Bubba, "because the principles it teaches don't change. Technology and marketing dynamics change almost daily, and you have to keep up with them. But God's wisdom on how to treat people doesn't change.

"Now just in case you're not quite as enthusiastic as I am about the value of biblical advice," says Zig Ziglar, another Atlanta native, "I encourage you to remember this. According to the April 28, 1986, issue of *Fortune* magazine, 91 percent of the CEOs of Fortune 500 companies apparently learned their values, ethics, and morals from the same source—the Bible and the church. At least they claimed affiliation with a Catholic or Protestant church or Jewish synagogue. (Less than 7 percent said they had no religion.)

"If W. Edwards Deming, Tom Peters, Warren Bennis, or Fred Smith had written a book that had positively affected the lives of 91 percent of the CEOs of Fortune 500 companies, you would undoubtedly head for the bookstore and pick up a copy."[5]

Find Your Weaknesses and Fix Them, **Ad Nauseam**

"We are adamant about continuous improvement," Dan emphasizes, "perpetually reinventing ourselves to maintain the edge required in this industry."

Case in point: In describing the company's new restaurant design, Kevin Salwen writes in the *Wall Street Journal*, "But this is more than just Chick-fil-A, Inc.'s 757th outlet to sell chicken. Instead, the brick-and-stucco store, with its huge wall murals and 16-foot-high indoor play space, is an emblem—a sign of the company's insistence on finding its weakest link and fixing it. And despite Chick-fil-A's 10 percent sales growth in existing free-standing stores this year—nearly triple the rate of the rest of the fast-food industry—the company is still scouring its business for things to change.

"Who should care? Virtually anyone looking for role models in business. 'The best companies are the ones that think they're doing a bad job, while the worst ones say, 'We're doing great,' contends Ken Bernhardt, a Georgia State University marketing professor in Atlanta and a consultant to the company."

The article concludes, "And next week, as the restaurant opens, Chick-fil-A customers run the risk of being trampled—by Chick-fil-A executives. 'A week after we're open, we'll be in there with the customers, asking "What do you like, what don't you like?"' says Mr. Robinson (senior VP of marketing). 'Then we'll tweak it.'"[6]

Each year an independent research firm surveys customers in each restaurant for the chain's customer satisfaction monitor, considered one of the most comprehensive report cards in the fast-food industry. Each year Chick-fil-A operators garnered feedback from thousands of one-on-one customer interviews.

HEART AND SOUL

Help Those Who Can't Help Themselves

The Cathys have a deep sense of obligation to the community, especially its young people. Their WinShape Centre Foundation provides scholarships and supports other youth-related programs. Camp WinShape hosts more than fifteen hundred kids each summer. The WinShape Homes program consists of eleven foster homes that provide long-term care in a family environment for more than one hundred children. Currently there are homes in Georgia, Tennessee, Alabama, and Brazil.

Their sponsorship of the Chick-fil-A Charity Championship, hosted by Nancy Lopez, on the LPGA tour has raised more than $2,000,000 for the program. A portion of the proceeds from the Chick-fil-A Peach Bowl sponsorship also goes to WinShape.

"When he's not tending to business, Cathy oversees a network of foster homes," writes Dan McGraw in *U.S. News & World Report.* "He says he would include more children were it not for unnecessary government red tape. 'The government can't always do it for us,' says Cathy. 'My philosophy is to put my money where it is the most useful (to the tune of $800,000 a year) and that place is these foster homes.'"[7]

Truett still works with the foster parents and selects the children for the program. He believes, "It's better to build boys and girls than to mend men and women."

Cultivate New Shoots from Old Roots

Family ownership can give a tremendous sense of continuity to a business. Yet any study of family-owned companies reveals lots of horror stories. "We are grateful for the unique relationship we've enjoyed through the years," remarks Dan, "not only among ourselves, but also with our executives."

Are there differences in management style between father and sons? Certainly. "Dad's not big on strategic planning or on meetings," says Dan. "He operates by his instincts, his street smarts. He *knows* what's going on with the business at the consumer level. We need his input as the next generation moves into leadership.

"Dad keeps a rigorous schedule. He's our best corporate spokesperson and still gives more than one hundred speeches a year. Both he and our COO, Jimmy Collins—who's been with us over thirty years—have done a marvelous job in growing from one diner to nearly nine hundred restaurants approaching a billion dollars in sales. They've done a lot to attract and retain top-caliber management. Many entrepreneurs can't make the radical changes I've seen them make over the years.

"It's critical to pay attention to the founder's core values," says Bubba, "and to make sure there's a good values match with the executives you bring on, especially during times of transition."

Bring Your Faith to Work

In the article quoted earlier, Furman Bisher notes the faith of the family patriarch. "He [Truett] looks not to himself as the main benefactor in his life but to a much higher influence that still shapes his world and the business policies of Chick-fil-A. Cathy's policy of operating six days a week and leaving the Lord's Day to be observed in worship, or whatever forms of leisure his employees choose, has been questioned. His firm stance has not wavered. 'We don't expect all our operators to be Christian,' he said, 'but we do expect them to operate on biblical principles. We have a diverse mixture in our crew, but we haven't had any conflict as far as our religious practices go.'

"At headquarters we have a devotional time once a week with about one hundred folks attending," says Bubba. "We have a music team and we sing and pray together. It's optional but Dad, Dan, Jimmy, and I make it a priority. At our corporate meeting in San Diego a few years ago, Dad gave each of our 700 operators a framed copy of Jeremiah 29:11: "'For I know the plans I have for you,' declares the LORD, 'plans to prosper you and not to harm you, plans to give you hope and a future.'" We believe this about Chick-fil-A."

"What wins the respect of other people is usually my father's accomplishments in business," Dan tells Jerry Winans in *Stand Firm*. "But the respect I have for my dad is based on the things people have not seen, stories that will probably never be told about him. If I can come close to being the father to my two sons he is for me, my brother, and my sister, I'll count my life as a success—no matter what happens to Chick-fil-A."[8]

SUMMARY OF KEY PRINCIPLES

- Pour a solid foundation of hard work.
- Find the right place for your business concept to blossom.
- Insist on superior quality in your signature products.
- Strive to satisfy every customer.

- Be a faithful steward of your people resources.
- Reward good management.
- Preserve the core; push the edge.
- Find your weaknesses and fix them, *ad nauseam.*
- Help those who can't help themselves.
- Cultivate new shoots from old roots.
- Bring your faith to work.

INFLUENTIAL BOOKS— RECOMMENDED READING

Dunn, David. *Try Giving Yourself Away.* Englewood Cliffs, N.J.: Prentice-Hall, 1970.

Hill, Napoleon. *Think and Grow Rich.* New York: Ballantine Books, 1950.

Sheldon, Charles. *In His Steps.* Grand Rapids: Zondervan, 1984.

Ziglar, Zig. *Over the Top.* Nashville: Thomas Nelson, 1997.

CHRISTOPHER A. CRANE was president and CEO of COMPS.COM, Inc., a leading commercial real estate information services and electronic commerce company until he sold it in 2000. He studied at the University of Vienna, Austria, and received his B.S. in finance *summa cum laude* from Boston College and his M.B.A. from Harvard Business School.

Crane bought COMPS in 1992 and took it public in 1999. Along the way he and his company have received several awards, including the 1999 Ernst & Young Entrepreneur of the Year Award and the Arthur Andersen Best Practices Award.

After COMPS had acquired thirteen companies, a larger company acquired COMPS in February of 2000. Chris now invests in rapdily growing technology companies and introduces successful entrepreneurs to ministries like World Vision, Youth With A Mission, Campus Crusade for Christ, and Impact Urban America.

Chris is a member of Young Presidents' Organization and MIT Enterprise Forum, and participates in Youth With A Mission's Homes of Hope, which builds houses for the poor in Mexico.

His avocations include tennis, skiing, and basketball. Together with his wife, Jane, and son, Andrew, he lives in La Jolla, California.

Chapter 13

THE ROAD TO AN IPO

"A successful business is just a series of problems successfully solved."
BUDDY KALB JR.[1]

When Chris Crane graduated from Harvard Business School in 1976 he was among the 1 percent of his class heading into entrepreneurial ventures. (Today the number is closer to 25 percent.) His first company failed, but he went on to cofound Graystone Capital Ltd. and to successful stints with Rotan Mosle (a Paine Webber subsidiary) and Oster Communications, Inc. Then in 1992 he acquired COMPS.COM, Inc.

"COMPS began in 1982," Crane recounts, "but the wife of its founder filed for divorce in 1992 and insisted on the sale of the company. At that time it generated $4 million in sales. I structured a deal to acquire the company with just $85,000 in cash, $50,000 of borrowed money, and another $125,000 of seller carry-back financing.

"While I got a $4 million company with only $135,000 in cash, the picture was anything but rosy. My projections showed COMPS would run out of cash in three months. It had lost money for five years in a row. At this time the commercial real estate industry in California was in the tank. Property values had dropped by half. Foreclosures and bankruptcies were rampant."

So why did Crane do the deal? What was he thinking?

Entrepreneur: Christopher Crane
Company: COMPS.COM, Inc.
    San Diego, California
Year Acquired: 1992
Acquisition Cost: $260,000
2000 Revenues: $20,000,000
    (when company was sold)
Employees: 400

TRUST AND OBEY

Know If and When to Buy

In a sense Chris Crane's purchase of COMPS was a case of following orders. He explains, "If you have an opportunity to buy a company, it may be intimidating, but regardless of how monumental it seems, give it consideration. Seek the Lord earnestly. If you believe this is something he wants you to pursue, be willing to step out in faith and try it. *Try* is the wrong word here. Buying a company is a lot like marriage. You can't just try it; you have to be *committed* to it if it's going to work.

"I have three pieces of advice for figuring out *if* and *when* to buy a company," Chris adds. "First, talk to knowledgeable people and get lots of counsel, especially from those who have bought and sold companies. Show them the deal, and listen to what they say. I asked twenty CEOs for advice, and fifteen told me not to buy COMPS. The five who had bought and sold companies themselves were the ones that thought the deal could make sense.

"When weighing advice, look at the backgrounds of those dispensing it. All twenty people I consulted were CEOs, but some had been hired; some were entrepreneurs who built their own company but hadn't bought other companies, and some had bought and sold companies before. I listened most carefully to the ones with experience relevant to my situation.

"My former boss, Merrill Oster, gave me some great ideas and even sent his CFO out for a week to help analyze the acquisition. They identified five business areas I needed to concentrate on and change, including increasing the sales force. Following their advice seemed like painting by the numbers.

"My most valuable advisor was my wife, Jane. She saw that the challenge was a fit with my skills. Without her encouragement and support, we would not have risked our life savings to buy a company that was losing money.

"Here's another piece of advice: determine if you have the makeup and constitution of a CEO. Some very good business people are Number Two types by temperament. Finally, as a Christian I believe in prayer and fasting to discern divine guidance."

Pray as Part of Planning . . . but Not in Place of Planning

Stressing the importance of this last point, Chris says, "I fasted Thursday night, all day Friday and Saturday, and got up early on Sunday with a pad and pen and my Bible. As I waited on the Lord, I got a sense of peace about the deal. He seemed to be telling me this would bring me to a new level of faith and spiritual maturity."

The need for prayer didn't stop with the purchase of COMPS. Chris recalls a time when "an $8 billion competitor began to focus on us and tried to knock us out. They dramatically lowered their prices—even below their costs—and improved the quality of their product. I lost a lot of sleep over that. But the founder of COMPS (still a minority investor) and I met almost weekly for prayer; it's one of the most important things we do. As we prayed about this situation, it ended up that the competitor called us one day and said this division was no longer important to them. They asked if we wanted to buy it? We did. I believe this development came about as an answer to prayer.

"I know Kevin Jenkins, the CEO of Canadian Airlines, a $3.2 billion company. He spends an hour a day with the Lord—twenty minutes praying about his schedule for the day, twenty minutes praying for family and friends, and twenty minutes reading the Bible. He says he gains back more than the time in effectiveness. I say to myself, *If someone who's running a $3.2 billion company can carve out an hour a day to pray, I can do the same thing.*"

Living by faith doesn't mean walking with your eyes closed. It's not trusting in feelings instead of facts. While Crane fasted and prayed for divine guidance, he also did his homework. "I spent three months doing due diligence on COMPS, working as much as sixteen hours a day. I talked to customers and competitors trying to figure out what was going on.

"Although I had limited cash, I spent more than $30,000 on legal fees. I used the best accountants and lawyers I could find to help structure the deal, including the most senior securities attorney with a large San Diego firm."

How did Crane feel about the risks involved? "When you start something of your own," he says, "there's tremendous energy in it. You have all these ideas flowing. It's one of the most invigorating times in life. It's also very scary—you may fail. You have to weigh the risks carefully.

"When we take a risk," writes economic consultant Peter Bernstein, "we are betting on an outcome that will result from a decision we have made, though we do not know for certain what the outcome will be. The essence of risk management lies in maximizing the areas where we have some control over the outcome while minimizing the areas where we have absolutely no control over the outcome and the linkage between effect and cause is hidden from us."[2]

IN HIS TIME

Determine If an IPO Is Right for You

"When I bought COMPS," Chris remembers, "I thought I would run it for ten or fifteen years and then sell it. The possibility of an IPO (initial public offering) first entered my mind in 1993, a year after I bought the company. At a trade association conference in New York, I heard a securities analyst speak about various information services companies going public. I realized some of them weren't much bigger than COMPS."

Is an IPO for everyone? "No," cautions Crane. "Many companies don't qualify. Also, the market has to be just right—the IPO window only opens at certain times. Even if you have a great company, you can't get out if the window is closed."

There's also the *P* in an IPO to consider. "When you're private you can be guarded with your financial and sales information," Chris states, "but once you go public, your customers and competitors have access to all this data. Also, the value of your stock isn't an issue when you're private, but when a public company's stock goes down, your investors, employees, and customers will want to know what's wrong.

"Then there's the loss of control. When I bought COMPS, I had total control because I raised all the money myself. This gave me a great deal of freedom to direct the business. I didn't have outside shareholders with different ideas on how the company should be run looking over my shoulder. When venture capitalists invested, I ensured they stayed below 50 percent voting power. When you lose voting control, the venture capitalists can toss you out of office and bring in a new CEO if business takes a downturn. With the IPO, I went from holding a majority of voting stock to a minority share."

So why go public? Crane sites several reasons. "First, to get the capital needed for growth. It can give you the twin currencies of cash and stock to acquire other companies. There's a great deal of consolidation occurring in most industries, and if you're not buying companies, you are likely to be bought yourself. Second, going public gives you credibility with customers and with strategic alliance partners such as larger companies. Third, it helps define your worth. We had already given stock options to our employees, but they really had no way to gauge the value of the options until we went public."

Do It Right If You Go Public

According to the numbers, when COMPS went public they did it right. Chris recalls, "We originally wanted to raise $40 million, which we thought quite ambitious. But our investment banker said to file for $50 million. By the end of our three-week road show—during which my CFO and I did six to nine presentations a day—we were twelve times oversubscribed and raised $67 million—an excellent response!"

Crane learned from experience that "the CEO serves as the primary architect of an IPO. He or she has to sell the story and sell the proposition to investment bankers and venture capitalists. The details can be arranged by the CFO, but the CEO has to be the front person. If the CEO can't get the message across, the IPO won't happen.

"Select the right advisors and investment bankers," Chris also advises. "Use an investment bank that specializes in your industry, and get them to commit to providing a securities analyst who will write reports about your stock on a periodic basis. And be sure to spend enough money and time to do it right. Our legal bills reached $500,000, and the accounting bills topped $250,000. You'll spend a tremendous amount of time with the accountants and attorneys and investment bankers going over every word in every line in the prospectus many, many times, so work with the best."

Most importantly according to Crane, "Spend time in prayer. The founder of the company and our senior vice president and I spent time praying about the IPO. It didn't look like a good market initially, but we got clear direction from the Lord to pursue the IPO. So as soon as the window opened again, we were ready for it ambitiously. Timing is very important on an IPO, and by God's grace—not our wisdom—we hit the market at its peak."

DAY BY DAY

Don't Let Cash Make You Dumb

"Completing an IPO is just the first mile in a marathon," says Crane. "You have this new capital to work with, but it comes with very high expectations from investors." He goes on to warn, "When you get a cash infusion, realize that cash can make you dumb. A cash infusion can fuel the tendency to spend more aggressively and less carefully than you should. You may start doing things like a big company instead of like an entrepreneur. I've watched businesses get large cash infusions and then lose their sense of urgency. They no longer have that entrepreneurial drive that came from having their backs to the wall financially."

Ben Cohen and Jerry Greenfield affirm the value of tight money. "Not having much money to start up actually helped us. A lot of people make the mistake of trying to start too high on the hog. They buy everything new instead of used, go first class all the way. Then the business fails because its debt load is too high. Entrepreneurs who get too much money too fast don't go through the bootstrapping stage. There's a lot of learning that happens in the early hands-on stages of a business. If we'd had money to throw at problems, we wouldn't have learned how to do things in the most cost-effective manner."[3]

Develop an Internet Strategy

COMPS started to grasp the power of the Internet in 1997 and 1998 when they bought a company that matched brokers' listings for commercial real estate with buyers. "Without our Internet strategy we wouldn't have been able to go public," Chris admits. "The Internet is revolutionizing the way most industries do business. Jack Welch, the chairman of GE, told his executives to look for ways to attack their business with new

Internet applications that made it better. He went on to say that if they didn't develop the new applications, people on the outside would—and would use them to take away business from GE."

Recruit Only AA Players for Your Team

"I have done something I picked up from a president of a company with about two hundred employees," Crane reveals. "No one in her firm is hired without her spending a few minutes with them. Same here, at least in our San Diego office where we had the major concentration of our employees.

"I tried to interview everybody over entry level and explain our philosophy to them. I did a lot of traveling because we were acquiring about one company a month, but having the right people was so important that I needed to stay involved in the process. I didn't do the initial screening. I only interviewed those whom my managers had already decided to hire. Ninety percent of the time I said OK.

"It used to take five applicants to get one good candidate. With the full employment market we had, it might have taken ten interviews, but it was worth it to find AA players. AA players are people who are good at what they do (aptitude) and who have a great attitude. And it doesn't stop with the initial hire. I've found AA players hire other AA players, and B players hire C players, so the effect becomes cumulative, for better or for worse."

HE LEADETH ME

Set the Example in Caring for Others

"While wealth is a gift of God," says Kenneth Kantzer, former editor of *Christianity Today*, "it is never a blessing if we keep it to ourselves."[4] "We who are living in this country and have been blessed materially have a huge opportunity and obligation that comes with wealth," Crane believes. "We have such a wonderful chance to reach our peers and to help the poor, and it's incumbent on us to do so.

"One of the most important things we did as a company was go to Tijuana twice a year to build homes for the poor. Our senior executive team, together with our families, would go in the spring, and then in

October we would go as a company and build several homes in a weekend. We paid our employees for Friday if they contributed their Saturdays.

"We worked with an organization called Youth With A Mission that coordinated our efforts. They made sure the foundations were poured and the tools and lumber were on site. Most of our employees said they enjoyed this and they felt tremendously rewarded in being able to have a positive impact on the lives of the less fortunate. These trips to Tijuana became part of our corporate culture."

Acknowledge Divine Providence

"To a great extent much of what has occurred at COMPS has been providential," insists the company's CEO. "It was providential I got control of a $4 million company with just $85,000 in cash and $50,000 of borrowed money. It was providential that Merrill Oster and his CFO, Tom Noon, spent time with me and helped me get the company turned around.

"It was providential I attended the Information Industry Association meeting in New York and had my eyes opened to the possibility of an IPO. At that same meeting an investment banker introduced me to summit partners who became our venture capitalist. It was very providential we went public at the peak time for Internet IPOs and that we sold the company a month before Internet stocks nose-dived.

"When the Lord calls you to do something bigger than you think you can handle, you have to be willing to go after it by faith. For me, stepping out in faith has meant a great deal of hard work and, frankly, a lot of anxiety. I wish I could say I've always had peace, but I haven't. There were many anxious nights right up until the sale closed. There are more opportunities ahead to depend on the Lord."

Now with the sale of COMPS, Chris muses, "Business is an important part of life, but it's just temporal. I want to continue to take risks by being involved in other activities that have eternal ramifications."

SUMMARY OF KEY PRINCIPLES

- Know if and when to buy.
- Pray as part of planning . . . but not in place of planning.
- Determine if an IPO is right for you.

- Do it right if you go public.
- Don't let cash make you dumb.
- Develop an Internet strategy.
- Recruit only AA players for your team.
- Set the example in caring for others.
- Acknowledge divine providence.

INFLUENTIAL BOOKS— RECOMMENDED READING

Christensen, Clayton M. *The Innovator's Dilemma.* Boston: Harvard Business School Press, 1996.

Downes, Larry, Chunka Mui, and Nicolas Negroponte. *Unleashing the Killer APP: Digital Strategy for Market Dominance.* Boston: Harvard Business School Press, 1998.

Oster, Merrill J. *Vision Driven Leadership.* San Bernardino: Here's Life, 1991.

Shapiro, Carl, and Hal R. Varian. *Information Rules: A Strategic Guide to the Network Economy.* Boston: Harvard Business School Press, 1998.

MICHAEL MANSON is a Scotsman at heart—by lineage, kilt, and family standard—but was born and raised in Phoenix, Arizona. He and his wife of thirteen years, Lyndel, still live in Phoenix with their three children and Bairn, his ninety-pound Bernese mountain dog.

He loves fishing and hunting and jokingly warns his partners that he once brought down a bounding wildebeest at 280 yards with one shot. The number and diversity of surprised animal heads mounted in his rustic home office seem to confirm his aiming acumen.

Michael did his undergraduate work at Stanford University and received his M.B.A. from Harvard Business School. He currently runs his own company, Brookstone Ventures, which is dedicated to helping promising and principled entrepreneurs. Most of Michael's business experience before Brookstone was with PETsMART, Inc.

Michael is active in the community through the Phoenix One Hundred Club, which helps the families of fallen police and firefighters, the Business Leadership Council, the Boy Scouts (being an Eagle Scout himself), and his church.

Chapter 14

IN SEARCH OF TRUTH

"Be an earnest seeker after the truth."
BILL ORR[1]

It requires uncommon vision, focused ability, and relentless drive to take a rough idea hatched in someone's basement and turn it into an international company with sales topping two billion dollars, all in about ten years. These qualities exemplify Michael Manson's leadership as a PETsMART cofounder.

PETsMART is a leading worldwide operator of superstores specializing in pet food, supplies, and services. The company opened its first store in Phoenix in March 1987. "We became operationally profitable in the first five months," remembers Manson, "rather remarkable from a retail standpoint."

The following year PETsMART opened five more stores. By 1992 they were opening over thirty stores annually. In 1993 more than fifty-three million American households spent $17 billion on pet food, supplies, and medical care. That same year, PETsMART went public and raised over $125 million in their initial public offering.

A retail maxim says success depends on "location, location, location!" In addition to serving on PETsMART's five-member executive committee, Manson was the senior vice president of real estate for almost a decade. During that time he secured some of the best retail real estate in the country. Most observers would acknowledge that PETsMART's success was built on the land Manson hunted down and bagged.

Entrepreneur: Michael Manson
Company: PETsMART
Phoenix, Arizona
Year Started: 1987
Start-up Costs: $1,500,000
1999 Revenues: $2,110,000,000
Associates: 21,000

SOLEMN QUEST

Live with Passion!

At six-foot-four, Michael is a big man. Those who know him will tell you the biggest thing about him is his passion. He lives passionately, works passionately, competes passionately, and follows his guiding principles passionately. These guiding principles truly define who he is and explain what he's been able to accomplish.

Effective leaders have an energetic drive to accomplish and a consuming ambition to succeed. While drive and ambition aren't unique to Michael, how he expresses them makes him special. He can tell you exactly where he's going and why. That's not just blind ambition. His target and his methods for getting there are clearly defined.

"The difference between raw ambition and passion," he explains, "is that raw ambition is rooted in a desire to advance oneself at any cost while passion is a desire to advance what one believes at any cost. A winner knows what to fight for and what to compromise on. A loser compromises on what he shouldn't and fights for what isn't worth fighting about. I am not worth fighting for, but the truth I believe in is worth fighting for."

So what *is* Michael passionate about?

"I am passionate about my God and about bringing favorable attention to him by the way I live the life he gives me. I am passionate about loving, protecting, and caring for my wife, Lyndel. I am passionate about loving my kids. I am passionate about my friends. I am passionate about succeeding with truth and with excellence."

The start-up days at PETsMART exemplify passionate commitment. Michael remembers working many twenty-four-hour days in some very primitive settings. "We would work around the clock, taking twenty-minute power naps to get by. Our desks were boards stacked on cinder blocks, and the rats outnumbered the people two to one. Vendors wouldn't sell to us because we were so new, but we fought through all the obstacles because we passionately believed the concept would work.

"Passion applied to entrepreneurial principles means staying focused on what's important," says Michael, "and beyond that, to know *why* something is important. Don't do anything halfway, and don't waste time in endeavors you can't be passionate about."

Seek the Truth, the Whole Truth, and Nothing but the Truth

Truth is not a particularly popular concept in some business circles. It requires diligence to discover, belief to apply, and commitment to maintain. Often expediency seems more efficient, but truth *is* the priority for Manson. Any serious discussion with him invariably involves a discourse on the central truth in his life. "There is nothing more important to me than finding the truth in every situation and then following that truth with all my heart."

This passion for truth creates an intriguing business style. "I seek integrity as a paramount requisite for anyone working with me in any capacity," Michael says. "Integrity means following through on commitments and promises. It means telling the good news and the bad news. It means telling the truth no matter what the repercussions might be."

One evidence of Manson's hunger for truth is his willingness to listen. "He will tell you what he thinks," one friend reports. "If you disagree with him, he will listen carefully to what you have to say, and he's willing to adjust his thinking when he finds that something you say is true."

Michael says, "If you focus on understanding what other people know and the truth they carry, as opposed to waiting for your turn to talk, you show honor and respect for the truth they know and that you can learn from them. At one time I worked for a large corporation whose president was a brilliant man with tremendous leadership capabilities, but he rarely listened to what others said. When you talked with him, he would interrupt halfway through a sentence and finish your thought with what he was thinking. For all his brilliance, I think he and the business eventually paid a terrible price for his inability to listen."

Manson reserves an honored place for truth in a world that often rejects even the possibility of truth. "I believe in objective truth because I believe there is a God who creates in truth and who reveals in truth. I believe Jesus was telling the truth when he said, 'I am the way and the truth and the life; no one comes to the Father except through me.' My life is built around the pursuit of truth, and that means my life is built around the pursuit of God. I have yet to find any conflict in the truth revealed in the Bible and the way things work in real life."

Michael concludes, "The principle of pursuing truth means being committed to integrity no matter what the consequences. It means always listening and always learning."

Speak the Truth in Love

For Michael, the natural corollary to seeking the truth is *speaking* the truth, with one critical caveat: speaking the truth *in love*. He defines *love* as "the perfect balance of all virtues, justice balanced with mercy; emotion with logic; strength with tenderness; discipline with playfulness; joy with reverence; trust with discernment. All these virtues are purified in the crucible of God's hand and in the furnace of trials and tribulation.

"I ask myself two questions before speaking my mind to another person," he says. "First, is my perspective on the situation really the truth, or is it tainted by my bias and agenda? Second, what is my motive for wanting to communicate this information? Am I angry? Do I want to intimidate, flatter, hurt, or manipulate this person to my own ends? If I can't honestly say my motive is to do good to the person, then I don't say it.

"How many businesses have failed, how many relationships have soured, how many friendships have been destroyed because perceived truth has been brutally delivered or not shared in love? Opinions, feelings, and emotions toward others often tend to masquerade as the truth in our own minds," Michael says. "A natural tendency is to filter the objective truth about others through the sieve of our own ambitions and experience. From there it's one small step to imposing our opinions as absolute truth. This is an especially dangerous tendency for those in positions of authority who can easily make the giant leap to 'might makes right.'"

Manson's commitment to speaking the truth in love expresses itself in a frank, nonthreatening openness with those around him. Those who know him affirm his consistency in speaking his mind but in an unthreatening way. "Michael continually reinforces the importance of trust and being loyal to each other," says a work associate. "He's up front with what he thinks but is careful to focus on the issues rather than the personalities. Good or bad, you know where he stands, and that makes it much easier to risk making a mistake, to stretch the envelope and move ahead quickly."

SMART MOVES

Honor Those in Authority

Manson is an astute and aggressive businessman who almost didn't go into business at all. He certainly wouldn't be where he is at today apart from God's plan for his life.

"I became a Christian in my junior year of Stanford," he recalls, "and I felt I should go into the ministry. But my father came out to school and said, 'I don't know much about the Bible, son, but I do know it commands you to obey your parents. And I say you can't go into the ministry until after you're a success in business.'

"I prayed and fasted for over two weeks and then submitted to my father's wishes. I asked the Lord to make me successful at business by the time I was thirty-five. I finished Stanford and, after helping my dad with his business, went to work for a company in Phoenix for the next two years."

Confident God would do his part, Michael concentrated diligently on what he could do. "I applied to Harvard Business School and I told my team at work—comprised of fifteen women—that if Harvard accepted me, I would wear a skirt to the office. The day after the call came inviting me to Harvard, I showed up in my kilt with full clan colors.

"It was during my second year of Harvard Business School that I uncovered the PETsMART concept. I was twenty-six. A friend put me on to Jim Dougherty, Ford Smith, and the PETsMART idea. I started reviewing the business plan and became impressed with the heart of Jim, the original founder, so I signed on. I flew back and forth to Phoenix on the weekends and did negotiations by phone. I became the senior vice president of real estate, in charge of real estate growth, property management, and construction."

Start Over If Necessary

"We started the first two stores and arranged for additional capital from Chancelor Management of Citibank, a real affirmation for us going forward. But the next year we had to completely restart the company because we ran out of cash and our investors wanted a more serious retail executive. We knew we needed more capital in order to grow. With retail, all your secrets are out on the trade floor. Consequently, you either grow fast and eat, or are eaten, because people can knock you off very quickly."

PETsMART managed to stay ahead of the pack. "By now we had nine units open," Manson remembers. "We had a Price Club mentality—stack it high, sell it low. We knew we needed a new executive officer to go to the next level. I found Sam Parker—whose vast experience included the Jewel Corporation—and proposed him to the board. Through a lot of rodeo riding, we got him to join PETsMART. Sam's a very capable, diligent guy, an earnest seeker after the truth.

"Together with Sam we brought in an additional $6.5 million in capital. We went back through the numbers, brought the executive team together with a design firm, and restructured our concept into generally what it is today."

SIMPLE TRUST

Let the Leaders Set the Pace

"Sam Parker was allowed to lead at PETsMART, and he worked through people like me," says Manson. "He allowed me to function almost autonomously. He gave me freedom and yet came alongside and supported me in different ways. With his encouragement we secured some of the best real estate in the U.S., and as a result we had a surprisingly low number of poorly performing stores.

"Jerry Gallagher, a board member and one of the brightest retail minds I've ever met, said to me as I was leaving PETsMART, 'Michael, you've been able to select more real estate more quickly and successfully, with fewer resources, than I've ever seen.' I owed this to Sam, who allowed me to really create and own the PETsMART process and to lead in my strengths for the good of the team.

"If you have great people around you with a sense of direction and inspired by truth," continues Manson, "let them set the pace and own the dream. I've learned from experience that what you *don't* want to do is hold back someone with ability for your own gratification or sense of control. Give the horse its head."

Make Transitions with Integrity

Paying attention to personal dynamics and internal relationships fueled external success. PETsMART grew exponentially, going public in 1993 and expanding its worldwide operations to over five hundred locations by 1998. While success was gratifying to Michael and very rewarding financially, he never lost sight of his passion to serve God.

"When I turned thirty-four, I read through my old prayer journals and realized how faithful God had been to me. I felt it was time for me to let go of PETsMART and look for other avenues of ministry. For me this involved getting released from my father's 'command' to stay in business. He actually brought the subject up when we were together at our cabin. He said, 'You've become a bigger success at business than I thought you could. I release you. Do what you want now.' This was right before my thirty-fifth birthday.

"The board asked me to stay on through April 1995 to complete our growth program and conclude several pending acquisitions, which I did. When I left PETsMART, I thought, *OK God, here we go. You and I are going to do great things in ministry.* But I was relying more on myself than on him and God pulled up my reins in an effort to call me back to him. What he was teaching me in this situation was to rely on him and to learn the truth that he loves me, not for what I do but for who I am in him.

"God says he is the great I AM, yet I was trying to prove myself by asking, 'Am I?' I was getting it reversed."

STRESS TEST

Face Life with Boldness and Courage

Being around Michael gives one a new appreciation for boldness and courage. "Don't be afraid," he says continually. "Don't second-guess yourself. Don't run yourself down in your own mind. Be a man. Be bold and courageous!" He frequently quotes these lines from Kipling's "If":
Be a man. Be bold and courageous!

If you can keep your head when all about you
Are losing theirs and blaming it on you . . . .
If you can meet with Triumph and Disaster
And treat those two impostors just the same . . . .
If you can force your heart and nerve and sinew
To serve your turn long after they are gone,

And so hold on when there is nothing in you
Except the Will which says to them: Hold on! . . .
Yours is the Earth and everything that's in it,
And—what is more—you'll be a Man my son![2]

Manson knows firsthand what these words mean. He began battling a mysterious and severe illness about two years into his PETsMART career. Within three weeks of leaving the company, the illness attacked with a ferocity that put him flat on his back for the better part of the next three years.

"The sickness progressed to a point where one morning my wife, Lyndel, found me motionless and feverish in bed," Michael recalls. "Unable to wake me and fearing the worst, she broke down and began praying. I could hear her, but I couldn't respond. Then I felt the presence of God working. The fever broke that afternoon. The next morning I went out in the yard and prayed. For the third time in my life, I became powerfully aware of God's presence in a most incredible way; beyond words to describe. I saw my purpose and resolved to carry it out with boldness and courage, no matter what the challenges might be."

The illness was finally diagnosed as a hyperimmune reaction to a toxin received from an insect bite. The two-year-long treatment required weekly infusions so strong they literally made Michael pass out every time he got one.

Trust God and Others with Your Life

"I can only surmise God allowed me to go through this experience to keep me from relying too much on myself," reflects Michael. "I learned how much I needed him and those he placed around me. I now enjoy a greater courage and boldness to do what I am called to do because I *know* I have a power backing me greater than any in this world."

Michael offers this advice to those facing life's challenges: "Don't back away from adversity. God works through our brokenness and vulnerability. Face problems head-on by relying on a power greater than yourself. Develop a close cadre of trusted friends, real soul mates you can rely on and pour your life into. I have about ten close friends I would go to the wall for. And they would go to the wall for me. We have committed to each other for the rest of our lives. We promised to take care of one another's families should anything happen to one of us. They are a great source of counsel, encouragement, and strength to me. And I hope each one of them knows the depth of my commitment to them, as well."

Unlike the cynical Ashleigh Brilliant, author of the book, *I Have Abandoned My Search for Truth, and Am Now Looking for a Good Fantasy*,[3] Michael Manson continues his quest for truth. His long-term staying power as an entrepreneur proves there are some basic aspects of success that can't be reduced to outward formulas and techniques. Success, as Michael Manson epitomizes it, is about living passionately, seeking the truth, speaking the truth in love, and living courageously for a higher purpose.

And that's the truth!

SUMMARY OF KEY PRINCIPLES

- Live with passion!
- Seek the truth, the whole truth, and nothing but the truth.
- Speak the truth in love.
- Honor those in authority.
- Start over if necessary.
- Let the leaders set the pace.
- Make transitions with integrity.
- Face life with boldness and courage.
- Trust God and others with your life.

INFLUENTIAL BOOKS— RECOMMENDED READING

The Holy Bible, New International Version. Colorado Springs: International Bible Society, 1973.

Aurelius, Marcus. *Meditations.* Amherst, N.Y.: Prometheus Books, 1991.

Lewis, C. S. *Mere Christianity.* New York: Bantam Books, 1983.

Pascal, Blaise. *Pensées.* New York, Penguin, 1995.

Redpath, Alan. *The Making of a Man of God: Studies in the Life of David.* Grand Rapids: Revell, 1994.

ESTEAN LENYOUN III is an entrepreneur, ordained minister, husband,
father, and man with a passion for the
inner cities. Born and raised in the inner
city of San Diego, he got his exit visa in
the form of an athletic scholarship to Long
Beach State University.

Recruited directly after college by IBM,
he served time with Big Blue, followed by
stints with Grubb & Ellis Commercial
Brokerage Company and Coldwell Banker. But at the same time he
was buying and selling real estate on his own. In the early 1980s, he
became president and CEO of Sun Peak Corporation (a master
planned community development company) with holdings in several states, including a large parcel in Park City, Utah, where some
of the events for the Winter Olympics of 2002 will be held.

Today he is the president and CEO of Impact Urban America—
a faith-based social entrepreneurial organization—as well as an
ordained associate pastor of Maranatha Chapel in Rancho
Bernardo, one of the largest churches in southern California. He
serves on the boards of several organizations, including Rosey
Grier's Giant Step and the Center for Faith Walks Leadership.

Estean enjoys public speaking, snow skiing (he's known as the
Black Avalanche in Park City), and keeping physically fit. He loves
spending time with his wife and ministry partner of over twenty
years, Karen, and his two sons, Hanson and Xavier. The Lenyouns
make their home in Scripps Ranch, California.

Chapter 15

DIAMONDS IN THE ROUGH

"We make a living by what we get . . . but we make a life by what we give."
WINSTON CHURCHILL[1]

Estean Lenyoun has always had a head for business. "I went to work at age
five," he remembers, "making twenty-five cents an hour pumping gas at my
father's Texaco station. I paid cash for my first car when I was twelve. But
southeast San Diego is a rough place to grow up, and it made a tough kid
out of me. By age ten I'd been kicked out of every school in the area. I car-
ried a switchblade and choke chain, street necessities, and became a leader
in the underworld of gangs and drugs."

An athletic scholarship to Long Beach State University opened up a
whole new future to Estean, one he quickly seized and made the most of.
Today he's one of the growing number of social entrepreneurs investing
their time and personal expertise in social and spiritual causes. Estean's
cause is the inner city—on the mean streets where he grew up.

HOME EQUITY

*Pursue Your Dreams While
Learning Your Trade*

After college Estean went to work
doing marketing for IBM. "But after
being corporate for a while," he says, "I
knew I wanted to be an entrepreneur,
not a company man. Eventually I left
and moved back to San Diego. I

Entrepreneur: Estean H. Lenyoun III
Company: Impact Urban America
   San Diego, California
Year Started: 1998
Start-up Costs: $150,000
1999 Revenues: $1,500,000
Employees: 100

bought a house in the inner city and later rented it out and bought another one. I built up equity and started learning about leverage. I realized the real estate market there provided some major opportunities, so I started Lenyoun Enterprises in 1974 and found tremendous deals on affordable housing. I acquired single and multifamily properties as well as raw land, and within two years I'd made my first million.

"This success motivated me to find out more about commercial real estate and I went to work for Grubb & Ellis Commercial Brokerage Company while keeping my own business going. My holdings constituted my safety net. I wanted to keep the *one* bird I had in hand while I searched for the *two* in the bush.

"I worked a lot of hours for Grubb & Ellis and expanded my own holdings at the same time. I became a principal on several large land deals and got involved with Master Planning Community Development in 1980. I believe I was the first minority master plan community developer in the country.

"For the next dozen years I had a great time and learned a lot of things, especially about financing. My own business evolved into Joint Venture Network, a company that connected the largest domestic developers with international sources of finance. At one point I had properties in five states, including prime units in Las Vegas, oceanfront property in Florida, a block in downtown San Diego, netting me an eight-figure personal worth."

Like many entrepreneurs, Lenyoun is seldom content to do only one thing at a time. "You can ride more than one horse," he believes, "as long as they're all going in the same direction. New businesses you add should be compatible with what you're already doing so they end up supporting each other." But there's a caveat. Estean warns of the danger of always switching to a faster mount. "If I would have stayed with my initial real estate holdings from the 1970s and early 1980s, I would have been much better off financially. I could have made more money with my original properties than I did by going through all those big land deals, office buildings, and warehouses because of the increased capital requirements and the risks associated with megadeals."

See Diamonds Where Others See Coal

Did keen foresight compel Estean to buy property in the inner city? "No," he candidly admits. "Initially, it was all I could afford. Only later did I realize it was all that most people could afford. There's a tremendous market for low-income housing. I found I could create great demand for my properties just by providing a bit of quality management. Plus, there was no competition. Others with the resources to acquire and manage these types of properties feared the neighborhoods and the neighbors. (The Watts riots in the 1960s had a lot to do with this.) But being a product of the inner city myself, I had a different perspective."

Estean quickly saw what others didn't. "I believe inner cities are acres of diamonds—businesswise, resourcewise, and ministrywise. I think they are one of America's best-kept secrets."

These same words appeared on the cover of the May 1999 issue of *Inc.*, which highlights "The Inner City 100"—entrepreneurial companies finding success in urban centers. In the lead article, "A Window on the New Economy," Michael Porter and Anne Habiby point out, "The average annual compound growth rate of the 100 companies on the list is 44 percent, and they collectively created 4,695 new jobs between 1993 and 1997."

The article details the size of inner-city markets. "The ICIC's (Initiative for a Competitive Inner City) research suggests that inner cities contain about 12 percent of all U.S. urban households . . . . More than 54 percent of workforce growth will come from minority communities, which are heavily concentrated in cities and inner cities . . . inner city residents annually contribute at least $85 billion, or 7 percent, of all U.S. retail spending. More than 25 percent of that demand is not being met by neighborhood retailers."

Porter and Habiby highlight the competitive advantages inner cities afford, including:

- a strategic location at the core of major urban areas, highways, and communication nodes;
- an underutilized workforce with high retention amid a tight overall national labor market;
- an undeserved local market with substantial purchasing power;

- opportunities for companies to link up with and provide outsourcing for competitive clusters.[2]

HIGHER CALL

Put God in His Place, and He Will Put You in Yours

Estean's elevator was on the way to the keyed floors at the top of the Hotel Success. "I had a knack for business and became a multimillionaire in my early thirties. I made a lot of money, worshiped it, and lost a lot of it. I had the corporate jet, homes in San Diego and Park City, and all the trappings. I dealt with large amounts of real estate, but I was also dealing in large amounts of alcohol and drugs. My family suffered because of my lifestyle, but I couldn't stop.

"Then things turned for the worse. The financial downturn in the market in the late 1980s made large land developments impossible to do, especially in Utah and California. Suddenly the money, the big house, and all the toys were gone. My marriage fell apart. Divorce seemed inevitable. Then a friend told us about Maranatha Chapel. We started going because I thought it would be good for the family. I listened to the messages and watched the lives of the people there. In 1991 I committed my life to Jesus Christ. He set me free from greed, materialism, alcohol, and drugs. He gave me life, and now I live to help others find freedom in him."

Lenyoun's rearranged priorities involved returning to his roots, not exactly the direction he expected. "The first thing I did when I became successful was to get out of the inner city. I never thought I'd go back. But the Lord has called me to apply what I've learned to help the people still trapped there. I understand what they go through. I know what the real problems are.

"You really have to be called to whatever social entrepreneurial endeavor you do. You have to count the cost before getting involved, and if you have a family, you have to make sure they are in 100 percent agreement with you."

Treat Your Background as an Asset Instead of a Liability

"Most folks who make it out of the inner city don't come back," Lenyoun says. "They figure, 'I'm in suburbia now. I have a great job. I make good money. The last thing I want to do is identify with my past.' So it has to be a God-thing to go back. It's definitely a call. In 1997, I spoke at a YPO (Young President's Organization) conference in La Jolla, California. Afterwards, Bill Bright asked to talk with me. We sat down together with another gentleman I'd never met named Bob Buford (see chap. 2). That meeting put a whole new twist on my life.

"At the time I was housing hundreds of people, and I planned to go into a full-time preaching and teaching ministry in the inner city. These men confirmed the gifts and calling I had for the city and fueled my desire to do something that could change the lives of the people there and also have a national influence. But they encouraged me to stay in the marketplace and use the gifts and experiences God had developed in me over the past twenty-some years.

"I realize now that the way we grow up and all of our life experiences are part of what God uses. Another part of the equation is our basic skills package, which I believe comes as a gift. We can fine-tune these skills and perfect our talents, but God gives us the basic package. Our job is to use all we have to do good in the world."

HEART DONOR

Consider Crossing Over to the Social Sector

Musicians sometimes "cross over" and try their talents in a different genre of music. Some entrepreneurs are doing the same thing, moving from the for-profit world to what Peter Drucker calls the "social sector."

Lenyoun has made the switch, influenced by one of his mentors, Bob Buford. "Bob refers to this as going from success to significance," Estean explains. "It involves taking the gifts, tools, and experiences God has given you and using them to benefit others. It means doing what you're good at for the causes you believe in. What keeps this crossover from happening more often is that entrepreneurs don't see involvement with nonprofit organizations or ministries as a viable investment of their time. They don't understand this sector because they haven't done their due diligence.

"A businessperson may look at nonprofit organizations and ministries and see their heart to help others," he continues, " but they also see that in most cases the people running them don't have the business expertise to get positive results. They have great desires and dreams, yet they often lack the knowledge and skill to run the ministry efficiently. Nonprofits may have the solutions to many of the problems in our communities, but they often lack the ability to implement them."

Before taking the plunge, Estean advises that entrepreneurs should test the waters. "I went on the boards of several community-based organizations for a few years to get a feel for what I was getting into. This is very important. You should make a thorough study of whom you're going to help. Learn all about their history, their track record, their credibility, and their passion."

Harmonize a Ministry Heart with a Business Mind

Lenyoun believes maximum effectiveness comes from harmonizing a *ministry heart* with a *business mind*. It's not surprising his heart and head are both captivated by the inner city. "Before my conversion," Estean says, "I'd been researching affordable housing, knowing this would be the wave of the future. I learned everything I could about it—sources of subsidy funding, low-income housing tax credits, etc. After finding Christ, I gained a new perspective on what I could do to make a difference. One thing led to another, and in 1992 Rosey Grier and I founded Rosey Grier's American Neighborhood Enterprises, a for-profit real estate development, rehab, management, and construction company. Our goal was to access the different types of government subsidies to provide affordable housing in the inner cities."

That company became the catalyst for another Christ-centered, faith-based organization Estean and Rosey started called Impact Urban America (IUA). IUA is the first nonprofit organization Estean has been involved in starting. "We have a vision to unite churches, communities, and corporations to rebuild the inner cities and urban centers of America. We want to transform urban America by developing practical, replicable models that include spiritual renewal, job and life skills training, and economic and business development for inner-city residents."

HELPING HAND

Equip Others to Succeed

All of Impact Urban America's programs are geared to empower people, not to foster dependency on others, especially not on the government. Estean decries what he calls neoplantationalism—"government programs and welfare handouts that keep people at a certain level of dependency. What the people are really looking for is tough love and accountability," he says. "They want hope and dignity, which must be earned. It can't just be given."

One of IUA's main efforts is their WORKS staffing program, among the first Christ-centered, inner-city staffing companies in the nation. It recruits, trains, and places temporary and long-term staff for local businesses. Estean spells out the core values of WORKS staffing: "To honor God in everything, to pursue continual self–improvement, to instill integrity, honesty, and respect for all ethnicities, classes, and creeds, and to cultivate civic virtue. We guarantee if one of our people doesn't meet an employer's expectation within the first four hours, there's no cost to the employer, and we'll provide a suitable replacement immediately.

"We are also looking at franchises as a way of tying all the pieces together," Lenyoun adds. "The goal would be for these employees to work their way into running the businesses and eventually owning them. The beauty of franchising is that we don't have to start from scratch, which has a high failure rate. We can partner with established companies like ServiceMaster and Mail Boxes Etc. (see chap. 10) in win-win relationships."

Speaking of ServiceMaster, their CEO, William Pollard, knows the importance of training people to succeed. He tells of the time several years ago when "the ServiceMaster board of directors had a two-day session with Peter Drucker. The purpose of our time was to review how we could be more effective in our planning and governance. Peter started off the seminar with one of his famous questions: 'What is your business?' The responses were varied and included the identification of markets we serve, such as our health care, education, and residential; and the services we deliver, such as food service, housekeeping, and maid service.

"After about five minutes of listening to the responses regarding our markets and services, Peter told our board something I have never been able to tell them. He said, 'You are all wrong. Your business is simply the training and development of people. You package it all different ways to meet the needs and demands of the customer, but your basic business is people training and motivation. You are delivering services. You can't deliver services without people. You can't deliver quality service to the customer without motivated and trained people.'"[3]

Go after the Mentors You Need

One key to good training is providing experienced mentors. The good ones are hard to find, and the more successful they are, the more inaccessible they become. But that hasn't stopped this former college football lineman from tackling those who can help him grow.

"I believe in seeking advice from people competent to give it," Estean says. "Once I identify someone I think can add to my life, I go after him. I did this with Ray Bentley, Bob Buford, Rosey Grier, Bob Kennedy, William Pollard, and Ken Blanchard. Being aggressive is definitely a key to getting through to successful people. Perseverance is one of the things this caliber of mentor looks for when deciding if they want to spend time with you. They figure if a simple no will turn you away like a puppy, they're not going to waste time with you. You can't run with the big dogs if you stay on the porch."

Howard Schultz, CEO of Starbucks, says the same thing. "Once you've figured out what you want to do, find someone who has done it before. Find not just talented executives but even more experienced entrepreneurs and businesspeople who can guide you. They know where to look for the mines in the minefield . . . . If one doesn't find you, beat the bushes till you find one who will take you on. And with the right mentor, don't be afraid to expose your vulnerabilities. Admit you don't know what you don't know. When you acknowledge your weaknesses and ask for advice, you'll be surprised how much others will help."[4]

The man who has been the most helpful to Estean is Rosey Grier, humanitarian and NFL legend. "As soon as I got my life straightened out and my priorities in line," recalls Estean, "the Lord gave me a *big* brother. Some friends told me I should meet with Rosey. We had a breakfast one morning, and we both knew immediately we were supposed to do something together. Initially we thought it would just be in San Diego, but in the more than eight years since then, our vision has expanded to the whole country.

"If I could change anything about my life," Estean reflects, "I would focus a lot earlier on my relationship with the Lord. Then I could have been doing what he wanted me to do a lot sooner and probably would have made a greater impact on more lives. But at the same time I wouldn't have had the experiences that make me who I am.

"I encourage anyone who has been blessed to reach out and help the unfortunate," he concludes. "Don't be afraid to touch the untouchable and love the unlovable. Take whatever you've been given, and use it to bless others. Jesus said, 'It is more blessed to give than to receive,' and I've found this to be so true in my life.

"I am a blessed man."

SUMMARY OF KEY PRINCIPLES

- Pursue your dreams while learning your trade.
- See diamonds where others see coal.
- Put God in his place, and he will put you in yours.
- Treat your background as an asset instead of a liability.
- Consider crossing over to the social sector.
- Harmonize a ministry heart with a business mind.
- Equip others to succeed.
- Go after the mentors you need.

INFLUENTIAL BOOKS— RECOMMENDED READING

Blanchard, Kenneth H. *The Heart of a Leader.* Tulsa: Honor Books, 1999.

Blanchard, Kenneth H., and Bill Hybels. *Leadership by the Book: Walking Your Faith in the Marketplace.* New York: William Morrow, 1999.

Buford, Bob. *Game Plan.* Grand Rapids: Zondervan, 1997.

———. *Halftime.* Grand Rapids: Zondervan, 1994.

Pollard, C. William. *The Soul of the Firm.* New York: HarperBusiness, 1996.

Born and raised in Oklahoma City, *KIRK HUMPHREYS* now serves as the city's mayor. He is also founder and president of two successful companies, Century Investments, Inc., and Century Asset Management, Inc. It's a good thing since his annual salary as mayor is only $2,000.

After graduating from the University of Oklahoma in 1972 with a degree in finance, Kirk and his brothers bought the family business from their father. After a rough start the business grew, and Kirk became financially independent before age thirty. However, he has not limited his activities to the marketplace. He served as a school board member for eight years before being elected mayor in 1998.

Humphreys serves as a member of the Oklahoma Municipal League and the U. S. Conference of Mayors. He is past president of the Putman City Board of Education, former chairman and board member of International Students, Inc., and of the Baptist Sunday School Board (now Lifeway). He currently sits on or chairs several city boards and commissions.

Kirk is an instrument-rated pilot and loves reading, snow skiing, and waterskiing. He and his wife, Danna, have three children and two Labrador retrievers and live in—where else?—Oklahoma City.

Chapter 16

PUBLIC SERVICE

*"It is as great and as difficult a spiritual calling to run the factories
and the mines, the banks and the department stores, the schools and
government agencies for the Kingdom of God as it is to pastor a church
or serve as an evangelist. There truly is no division between sacred
and secular except what we have created."*

DALLAS WILLARD[1]

Oklahoma City is the largest city in Oklahoma, with 460,000 residents and more than a million people in the metro area. It is the twenty-eighth largest city and the forty-sixth largest metropolitan area in the U.S. Its current mayor is an entrepreneur with "five-and-dime" roots.

"My dad is a classic entrepreneur," says the Honorable Kirk Humphreys. "All my growing-up years he worked with variety stores—five-and-dimes—until the 1950s when he got into the wholesale end of the business, selling everything from hair care accessories to pet supplies to sewing notions.

"During the 1960s he focused almost exclusively on army and air force exchanges. In the early 1970s he sold the company to my older brother, Kent, and me, and seventeen months later most of the business had disappeared. The military exchange services were cutting out wholesalers like us. We scaled down our operation and started calling on the civilian market, where we were virtually unknown. By 1974 we'd dropped from thirty employees to four."

Entrepreneur: Kirk Humphreys
Oklahoma City, Oklahoma
Company: Oklahoma City Mayor
1999 Revenues: $677,000,000
Employees: 4,500

Rather than quit, the Humphreys boys determined the only way to go was up.

PERSONAL SUCCESS

Escape the Complacency That Can Come with Success

Kirk recalls, "By 1974 there were three brothers involved in Jacks Service Company (my father's name is Jack). Each of us had a van and we hit the road. My written goal in January 1974 was to double sales from $15,000 to $30,000 a month, still a far cry from the $125,000 my father had been doing. But we made it by the end of the year, and the next year we bought another company. It turned out to be the first of fifteen companies we purchased over the next fifteen years. We increased our product line by buying out competitors. When we added ethnic health and beauty aids, our business exploded, and we jumped from $2 million a year in sales in 1977 to $24 million in 1984.

"I graduated from college with a goal to reach a net worth of a million dollars," Humphreys says. "I did that by age thirty. I was very successful and enjoyed my work and my life. But one day, May 3, 1989 to be exact, I woke up at 2:30 in the morning and couldn't go back to sleep. I got out of bed and tried to figure out what was bugging me. It came down to the fact that after seventeen years I felt like I'd done everything I knew to do in this line of business. I'd lost the sense of challenge.

"I couldn't remember a day in my life when I didn't want to get up and go to work. I would rather work than eat. But not anymore. So I sat there and wrote out the pros and cons of selling my share of the company. At the time I was making great money. I had a Mercedes for a company car and six weeks of paid vacation a year. What's not to like about a job like that? But on my list I came up with three reasons to stay and about a dozen reasons to sell. I made my decision before dawn."

Make Life Transitions with Care

"Being in business is not about making money," says entrepreneur and author Paul Hawken. "It is a way to become who you are."[2] Humphreys wasn't ready to stop growing just because he was making a lot of money.

Still, not wanting to be rash, he came up with a way to test his sense of direction.

"I decided to go four months without saying a word to anyone except my wife," says Kirk. "I didn't even tell my father or brothers. I wanted to make sure I didn't do something I'd regret." Confirmed in his own heart by the end of the time, Kirk approached his brothers and told them he wanted to sell out. "I gave them two months notice and worked another two months before concluding the deal."

Now what? "The ministry of the Navigators has had a great impact on my life since college," Kirk says, "and I always assumed God would lead me into full-time ministry if I ever got business out of the way. Well, I cleared the decks vocationally, but nothing happened. Direction into the ministry never materialized, and I finally realized that I'm a businessperson. It's what I enjoy, what I'm good at. It's what God wants me to do."

At the same time Kirk sold his stake in Jacks Service Company to his brothers, he bought their shares of Century Investments, a real estate company they had been doing on the side for years. "It's not a huge operation," says Humphreys, "but since 1989 I've put together thirteen different limited partnerships in seven states across the Southwest and Southeast. With only three employees I've been able to handle or develop more than forty-five properties and generate $5 million in revenue in 1998. I've also had a lot of freedom to do other things."

What kind of other things?

PUBLIC SERVICE

Pursue Fresh Challenges Outside of Business

"In 1982 I ran for the school board in our suburban school district, the third largest in Oklahoma, with almost 18,000 students. I lost by thirty-seven votes, but in 1987 I ran again, got elected, and served for eight years. As a Christian I felt I needed to be involved in the world where I lived instead of complaining about it.

"A lot of my Christian friends were pulling out of the public schools and sending their children to private schools. I have no problem with that, or with home schooling. If I lived three blocks from where I do, I would be homeschooling. Children are different and situations are different. Still, I wanted to do something within the system. I really enjoyed my time on the board and believe I helped make a difference."

Make a difference simply by serving on a school board? Absolutely. Former Solicitor General and Supreme Court nominee Robert Bork says, "Perhaps the most promising development in our time is the rise of an energetic, optimistic, and politically sophisticated religious conservatism . . . . Though these conservatives can help elect candidates to national and statewide offices, as they have repeatedly demonstrated, their more important influence may lie elsewhere. Because it is a grass roots movement, the new religious conservatism can alter the culture both by electing local officials and school boards (which have greater effects on culture than do national politicians), and by setting a moral tone in opposition to today's liberal relativism."[3]

Follow Your Sense of Calling, Even to Unexpected Places

After resigning from the school board in 1995, Kirk planned to focus on his family, his business, and his church, First Southern Baptist of Del City. "I was burned-out on the public sector," he says. "Then on January 16, 1997, Kay Dudley called me. She's the director of appointments for Governor Frank Keating and is very politically connected. She talked to me about running for mayor of Oklahoma City. Kay said she had been praying about the mayoral race, and God kept bringing my name to mind.

"I told her no every way I knew how, and she finally asked if I would talk to my wife and pray about it over the weekend. So I went home, certain Danna would say to forget it. Instead she said, 'I think it's a wonderful idea. You would do a great job!' As I prayed and read Scripture, I kept coming across verses like Proverbs 11:11: 'Through the blessing of the upright a city is exalted.'

"On Monday, back at the office, I got a call from my pastor, Tom Elliff. At that time he served as president of the Southern Baptist Convention. He called from a plane. When I told him about Kay Dudley's request he said, 'For some time I've been praying that one of four men would run for mayor, and you are one of the four.' That blew me away!

"Four days later I decided to run for mayor. The election was less than eight weeks away. I did some polling and learned that 90 percent of Oklahoma City's residents had never heard of me. I was running against three sitting city council members who all had great name recognition. I hired the best political consulting firm in this part of the country. We put together a great campaign and spent a whole lot of money. I got 46 percent of the primary vote and in the runoff election a few weeks later, I received 68 percent of the vote.

"Running for mayor wasn't something I thought I would ever do," Kirk muses, "but it became something I felt called to do."

PRACTICAL CONCERN

Give Your Time and Talents to Causes You Believe In

The educational and political sectors aren't the only arenas where Humphreys has invested his time and talents. For almost ten years he served on the board of International Students, Inc. Headquartered in Colorado Springs, ISI has field staff in more than 130 cities across the U.S. serving more than 320 campuses. Their mission is to reach the over half million international students studying in the U.S. with the good news of Jesus Christ.

"I've always been captivated by ISI's vision of befriending and evangelizing students while they're in this country," says Humphreys, "then discipling and equipping them to go back and impact their home countries. It's by far the cheapest and most effective way to do foreign missions."

At one point the ministry experienced severe internal troubles, and the board asked Kirk if he would give ISI three days a week for six months. They asked him to commute to Colorado Springs and become interim executive vice president. Kirk agreed, often making the trip in his own plane.

"I had enough sense to know not to go into the situation without the authority to make it work," he states with the voice of experience. "I agreed to help on three conditions. Number one: six months only. Number two: I wasn't a candidate for a permanent position. Number three: I would function as chief operating officer with absolute control over personnel. I could

hire or fire anyone I wanted, including rehiring key personnel who had just resigned.

"I don't mind facing problems head-on when it's necessary. By my third day at ISI, it became apparent the president, a friend of mine, needed to resign, and I told him so. It took about a month to convince him, but he ultimately did. Overall it was a very tough assignment, and by the end of that six months I was worn out. The ministry is doing well today and changing a lot of lives. I'm very thankful to be a part of that."

Live for Something Bigger Than Yourself

What would motivate a busy businessman to spend so much time and energy on rescuing a ministry? Humphreys says, "It's a matter of believing and investing in causes that are bigger than your own well-being. Helping ISI took me away from my business and my family. It wore me out physically. But the irony is that I prospered financially that year. My business did very well even though I couldn't spend much time on it. God took care of me.

"The same goes for getting involved in public life," he continues, "whether it's city, state, or federal government. I consider it a privilege to be mayor and to have an impact on the city where I've lived for forty-eight years. I can help improve our neighborhoods and the quality of life for future generations. That's a real privilege.

"What do you do with your life after your needs are met?" Humphreys asks. "You can devote yourself to business and stack up more money. Or you can give your life over to pleasure and play all the fine golf courses or chase all the beautiful women in the world. Or you can invest yourself in helping others and improving the world. Which do you suppose will make more sense after you're dead?"

PRODUCTIVE LIFE

Ensure Future Freedom through Hard Work

Kirk believes, "Being involved socially is part of a balanced life. True, not everyone can afford to work in the public or nonprofit sectors even if he or she wanted to. My situation is unusual in that I can work on a job paying $2,000 a year, but I hardly live a pauper's life.

"The reason I can serve now, largely at my own expense, is that for many years I lived well below my means and focused on building up my savings and investments. Too many business people spend money as fast as they make it. If the flow ever stops, they'll be in trouble because they haven't built up any equity. What you do with the dollars you earn now largely controls the range of options you'll have later in life.

"My counsel to businesspersons today is simple. Get your lifestyle under control so you can give your life to something more than making a living. The Bible says there is a time to plow, a time to nurture, and a time to reap. The problem with a lot of people is they're busy having a good time in their twenties when they ought to be working hard. Then in their late forties, when they should be reaping, they're still having to plow."

According to Zig Ziglar, "The profile of a wealthy person is this: hard work, perseverance and most of all, self-discipline. The average wealthy person has lived all his adult life in the same town. He's been married once and is still married. He lives in a middle-class neighborhood next to people with a fraction of his wealth. He's a compulsive saver and investor, and he's made his money on his own. Eighty percent of America's millionaires are first-generation rich."[4]

Dare to Be a Daniel

Humphreys knows that with wealth comes the opportunity and the responsibility to serve. "I spend about a day a week on my private business, and the rest of my time is taken up being mayor," he explains. "In our system we have a city manager who really runs the city. He has forty-five hundred employees. I have two. I chair the city council of eight members, and I have a lot of appointee powers to boards and commissions. But I'm not the dictator of the city; I'm just the chief spokesman and arm twister. If I can't get four other council members to go with me, I have nothing."

Involvement in politics is anything but easy, yet Kirk draws inspiration from biblical role models like Joseph and Daniel. "I did a talk recently on the life of Daniel. I pointed out that Daniel had a *visible* faith. He prayed three times a day toward Jerusalem with the windows open. Everyone knew they could look in there and see him praying. His faith was public and predictable, which helped make him believable. Later in life, when he survived the lion's den, the king put out a decree honoring Daniel's faith and Daniel's God. People in the real world saw his faith and were impacted by it."

Humphreys points out that one of the sources of Daniel's strength came from a small group of close friends. "I believe it's important for everyone to have a small group of peers from whom they can draw support and with whom they can be totally transparent. I have a few friends I meet and pray with weekly, and they've been a great help to me through the years.

"We all need a few people who know and love us and who will tell us what we need to hear. When we're in the heat of battle and under pressure, we need people nearby we can trust. Too many successful people are isolated from this type of relationship, which makes them vulnerable.

"The way I have chosen to live out my faith and express who I am includes being salt and light where I live. Right now this involves being mayor. Who knows what's next?"

SUMMARY OF KEY PRINCIPLES

- Escape the complacency that can come with success.
- Make life transitions with care.
- Pursue fresh challenges outside of business.
- Follow your sense of calling, even to unexpected places.
- Give your time and talents to causes you believe in.
- Live for something bigger than yourself.
- Ensure future freedom through hard work.
- Dare to be a Daniel.

INFLUENTIAL BOOKS— RECOMMENDED READING

Clason, George S. *The Richest Man in Babylon,* New York: Penguin, 1972.
Colson, Charles W. *Loving God.* Grand Rapids: Zondervan, 1996.
Lewis, C. S. *Mere Christianity.* New York: Macmillan, 1952.

Mandino, Og. *The Greatest Salesman in the World.* New York: Bantam Books, 1983.

Piper, John. *A Godward Life: Savoring the Supremacy of God in all Life.* Portland: Multnomah Press, 1997.

JACQUELINE BACA is the third of five children born to a family with deep roots in New Mexico. A native of Albuquerque, she holds a bachelor's degree in political science and an M.B.A., both from the University of New Mexico. She is committed to helping provide educational and job opportunities to disadvantaged and minority persons through her business activities as president of Bueno Foods and through her community service.

In 1994 Jackie was named U.S. Hispano Chamber of Commerce Businesswoman of the Year and the Albuquerque Hispano Chamber of Commerce selected her company as the Small Business of the Year. In 1996 she was inducted into the University of New Mexico's Anderson Graduate School of Management's Hall of Fame.

Baca has served on the boards of St. Joseph's Hospital, the Rio Grande Development Corporation, the University of New Mexico Entrepreneur Advisory Board, Executive Women International, and the New Mexico Joint Economic Development Initiative.

Jackie enjoys the peace and quiet of early morning walks. She likes to hike in the great outdoors. She's an avid reader with a passion for biographies and motivational books. Together with her husband, Ken Genco, she makes her home in Corrales, New Mexico.

Chapter 17
¡LA FAMILIA BUENA!

*"People will not look forward to posterity who never
look backward to their ancestors."*
EDMUND BURKE[1]

Jackie Baca runs one of the oldest food companies in New Mexico and one of the nation's largest Hispanic-owned businesses. El Encanto, Inc. (d/b/a Bueno Foods) prepares and distributes more than 150 authentic Mexican and New Mexican food products to restaurants and retail outlets in nearly all fifty states.

It all began with Ace Food Store, started by brothers Augustine, Raymond, and Joseph Baca in 1946 in Albuquerque's South Valley. In 1951 they incorporated, and Joe became the company's secretary-treasurer and, later, its second president. It took more than twenty years to reach the $1 million sales mark and another dozen years to reach $5 million.

In 1986 Joe's daughter, Jackie, became the third president of Bueno Foods, and things really started to heat up. Under her leadership, sales, profits, and employment have increased fivefold. In managing the transition to a modern, growth-oriented business, she has recruited professional middle managers, installed automation, and guided product and trade name development.

Not bad for someone who never expected to follow in her father's footsteps.

Entrepreneur: Jacqueline Baca
Albuquerque, New Mexico
Company: Bueno Foods
Year Started: 1951
Start-up Costs: $4,000
1999 Revenues: N/A
Employees: 250 (plus 300 seasonal workers)

JOE'S KID

Work Your Way into Leadership, Even If Your Name Is on the Door

"Together with my siblings and cousins I worked in the business as I grew up," remembers Jackie. "My first real job was in the meat department making tamales. From there I moved to production and then sales. I've headed boxing crews, done grocery-store demonstrations, done clerical, credit, and collection jobs, and at one point even selected our first computer system. It was a family joke. My dad would give me anything anybody else didn't want to do, and he'd say, 'Try it! It'll be a good experience.'

"My coworkers didn't initially welcome me with open arms. After all, I was the boss's daughter. I had to prove myself. I worked hard, and I made many friends. Some still work for us. When I finished my undergraduate degree in political science, I took a year off before going to law school and returned to Bueno full time. I just loved it and saw so much potential. So I decided to get an M.B.A. instead.

"I worked at Bueno while earning my degree," continues Baca, "and felt lucky in that my dad let me dig in and experiment. As I proved myself, he listened to my new ideas. Still, I never planned to make a career of the family business. I assumed after getting my M.B.A. I would find a 'real' job, then perhaps return later."

Just how helpful was the book learning? "A formal education in business management teaches you a language," Jackie told the *Albuquerque Journal.* "The accounting helps, too, but it is the lingo—of economics, accounting, marketing, statistics—that gives you enough exposure to ask the experts working for you the right questions.[2] However, my real training began in 1980 when I started working side by side with Dad."

Put Yourself on the Line for Your Ideas

"At that time we had several locations throughout the city, and inventory control was a nightmare," Baca continues. "I talked my dad and uncle into building a larger plant and consolidating. Our first attempts at financing failed; almost every bank in the city turned us down. Finally I helped structure a creative financing package that included money from HUD's

Urban Development Action Grant Program. But in order to approve the funding, lenders wanted continuity of leadership and asked me to guarantee the debt along with dad.

"I agreed to stay at Bueno, and we got the money. I became executive vice president, responsible for building the new facility and generating the sales to make the expansion successful. I had to make sure all those great projections I put together became reality. What an awesome responsibility for someone in her twenties! Some might say I had vision. I think it was naïveté. If I knew then what I know now, I'm not sure I would have agreed."

Jackie muses, "My dad had a lot of faith in his children and was very open to my coming in and bringing new ideas. However, we also had our differences. I took a radical approach to the business because I knew we needed aggressive growth. And just as with the employees, I had to earn the respect of my father's management team—all men much older than me. It really helped when my younger brother came on board after completing his law degree at Harvard. He took over operations, and I concentrated on strategic planning, sales, marketing, finance, and public relations. I love problem solving, although sometimes it can be relentless.

"My dad got cancer and died in 1989 at age sixty-five. It was a real shock. Still, I had worked with him daily for ten years and been president for four years, so we were as prepared as we could be for the transition from first- to second-generation leadership."

FAMILY CIRCLE

Build on Strengths Where Family Is Involved

"We are a family business and a business family," says Jackie. "We enjoy working together, and each of us has our own area of expertise. My brother, Gene, is vice president and handles operations. My mother, Marie, joined Bueno after retiring from over thirty years in elementary education. She helps in HR with training and hiring. My older sister, Catherine—a medical doctor with degrees in biology and public health—oversees technical services, including quality control and research and development. My younger sister, Ana, works in marketing. Being close as a family gives us important advantages."

Futurist Alvin Tofler would agree. In *Powershift*, he points out one of the strengths of a family business:

Today's resurrection of small business and the family firm brings with it an ideology, an ethic, and an information system that is profoundly antibureaucratic. In a family, everything is understood. By contrast, bureaucracy is based on the premise that nothing is understood. (Hence the need for everything to be spelled out in an operational manual and for employees to work "by the book.") The more things are understood, the less has to be verbalized or communicated by memo. The more shared knowledge or information, the fewer the cubbyholes and channels needed in an organization.

In a bureaucracy it is often difficult to know who has power, despite the formal hierarchy, and titles. In the family enterprise, everyone knows that titles and formality don't count. Power is held by the patriarch or, occasionally, the matriarch. And when he or she passes from the scene, it is usually conferred on a hand-picked relative.[3]

School Yourself for the Benefit of Others

Both of Jackie's parents were teachers before organizing Bueno Foods, and they placed a premium on a good education. The Baca children have degrees from the likes of Harvard (Gene and Catherine), the University of Michigan (Marijo), the University of New Mexico (Jackie), and Stanford (Ana). But the most important education they received came from home.

"My folks were devout Catholics," Jackie says, "and the way they lived set a great example for us kids. They always did right by people and taught us to do the same. They raised us to believe we were put on earth to serve others. They encouraged us to go into helping professions but let us make our own choices.

"In pursuing my political science degree, I came to realize what a helping profession business could be. When you create jobs, you give people an opportunity to better themselves. Work gives people dignity and the means to improve their lot in life. What a noble calling!

"The value of a man resides in what he gives," said Albert Einstein, "and not in what he is capable of receiving. The most important motive for study at school, at the university, and in life is the pleasure of working and thereby obtaining results which will serve the community."[4]

GOOD NEIGHBOR

Improve People's Lives as Part of Your Mission

"After my dad died we decided to put our mission statement and core values into writing," Jackie recalls. "We found this surprisingly easy to do because we had seen these modeled by our parents all our lives. Our purpose is to have a positive influence on people's lives through our products and our organization, and one of our core values is the belief that a responsible and profitable business contributes to the well-being of society. Profit is not our sole goal, but it is a means for us to contribute to society and to provide security for the Bueno family.

"A major way we do this is by creating jobs. My dad and his brothers started Bueno Foods in the first place because jobs were scarce after World War II, especially for Hispanics. They wanted Bueno to provide work for the unemployed and underemployed, thereby making a difference, which it has. We've gone from 25 employees in 1967 to 250 employees and 300 seasonal workers today."

Bueno directs its hiring emphasis toward minorities and the disadvantaged, especially from the Barelas and South Valley areas. Skin color, gender, or language aren't barriers to employment. Once hired, the company provides educational and advancement opportunities and offers benefits such as flextime, health insurance, and a 401K retirement plan with matching contributions. Bueno estimates more than a thousand employees have received college degrees or trade-school diplomas with the help of school-friendly scheduling.

The Baca passion for education is why the company has instituted the Raymond J. Baca and Joseph J. Baca Scholarships for minority high school seniors and contributed to the University of New Mexico Presidential

Scholarship Fund. They also participate in the Greater Albuquerque Chamber of Commerce Join-a-School Program.

Bueno invests 4 to 6 percent of pretax profits in contributions and donations to their community. "We grew up here," reflects Jackie. "We went through the local schools in a poor part of town, and one of my favorite things to do is to talk to students about business. My Hispanic background is similar to theirs, and I can be a role model to them."

Expand Production Capacity without Compromising Product Quality

"My family was among the first to commercialize Mexican and New Mexican foods," Baca says, "and we struggled to establish a market. Now Southwestern food is very popular. To meet customer demand we are expanding our product line and geographic distribution area, but not at the expense of authenticity.

"Many of our products are based on family recipes from my grandmother, mother, aunts, and uncles. As we grow, we remain passionately committed to preserving the taste of genuine New Mexican cuisine in the transition from home recipes to commercial products.

"We have the best of both worlds," Baca says with pride, "authentic food from a family-owned business prepared with the sophistication of a large, modern company. We have the flexibility of a small company combined with a state-of-the-art quality control department and a research-and-development team that focuses on nutrition and continual product improvement.

"We process millions of pounds of green chile, red chile, and frozen products each year using state-of-the-art methods," says Baca. "We were one of the first to develop commercial equipment to flame roast and freeze green chile. We also developed an automated system to stone grind red chile and corn in a way that remains true to our traditions. We spend a lot of time determining our product mix, retiring items that don't meet certain goals, and introducing new products that fit consumers' tastes and lifestyles. We also work hard on our packaging to present the right image."

HOME ECONOMICS

Protect the Environment as Standard Operating Procedure

Jackie believes the key to small business success is *managed growth*. Not so fast as to throw life out of whack and not so slow as to sink into the status quo. It's her job as president to find the balance.

Another area where balance is important to the Bacas is maintaining the equilibrium between economics and the environment. "We feel a sense of duty to the environment and strive to minimize our impact on it," Jackie explains. "My brother and sister both have biology degrees, and they are very concerned about environmental issues. For years all of the corn and tortilla scraps from our operation have been given to area pig farmers.

"We reuse 50 percent of the cardboard boxes we receive, and often when salespeople deliver products, they bring back the boxes. Nearly all of our product packaging is recyclable. During our 1990 expansion we spent a lot of money to install wastewater treatment equipment to remove food particle before water is discharged into the city system.

"We live here, too, and keeping the environment clean is one of our contributions to ourselves, our community, and our children."

Assume Others Want to Do the Right Thing

It may seem naïve, but Jackie believes others want to do the right thing. "People often get into trouble if they don't," she says. "I notice distrust causes a lot of conflicts and unnecessary grief. I choose to assume that people usually try to do what's right. I choose to trust people. This helps me when dealing with employees, suppliers, and customers."

Trust breeds integrity. As Bruce McNicol, president of Leadership Catalyst says, "Integrity provides the opportunity to teach truth and love others, the essence of positive influence."[5] When you trust people you develop a reputation for integrity, which is a priceless asset in business. Plus, companies that model integrity attract people with integrity.

Jackie's trust comes from her choice to see others as moral and spiritual beings, not simply as employees, or customers. Tom Chappell, cofounder and CEO of Tom's of Maine, says, "In the business of managing time, money, and people, it's essential that spirituality be step one. Spirituality says the world is bigger than our balance sheet, bigger than the walls of Tom's of Maine. You have to be intentional about integrating spirituality with business. That's what our mission does. Our statement of beliefs says, 'We believe that both human beings and nature have inherent worth and deserve our respect.'"[6]

The moral foundation at Bueno Foods comes from the Baca family. Homemade recipes and Christian values served up by children following their parent's example. Old-fashioned traditions and modern technology blended to create a national business with neighborhood concerns.

"Family is so important to us," Jackie repeats. "Our roots in New Mexico go back over four hundred years. We are proud of our heritage and love to share it with our customers through Bueno Foods. As a family we work together, play together, laugh and cry together, and do what we can to help our neighbors together. This togetherness is one of the best things about my life.

"I think dad would be proud of what we are doing with the company he started almost fifty years ago. I know we are proud of him."

SUMMARY OF KEY PRINCIPLES

- Work your way into leadership, even if your name is on the door.
- Put yourself on the line for your ideas.
- Build on strengths where family is involved.
- School yourself for the benefit of others.
- Improve people's lives as part of your mission.
- Expand production capacity without compromising product quality.
- Protect the environment as standard operating procedure.
- Assume others want to do the right thing.

INFLUENTIAL BOOKS— RECOMMENDED READING

Collins, James C., and William C. Lazier. *Beyond Entrepreneurship: Turning Your Business into an Enduring Great Company.* Parmus, N.J.: Prentice Hall, 1995.

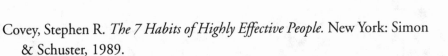

Covey, Stephen R. *The 7 Habits of Highly Effective People.* New York: Simon & Schuster, 1989.

Machiavelli, Niccolo. *The Prince.* New York: Bantam Classics, 1984.

Maxwell, John C., and Jim Dornan. *Becoming a Person of Influence: How to Positively Impact the Lives of Others.* Nashville: Thomas Nelson, 1997.

ROBERT FULTON grew up outside Boston and paid his dues in the school of hard knocks. He is the founder and past president of Web Industries, which has received numerous awards and write-ups in magazines like *Inc.* and *U.S. News & World Report* for its innovative approach to business and exemplary care of employees. This success creates a bully pulpit for Fulton, who shares his business acumen with entrepreneurs around the world.

Since his semiretirement in 1991, he has traveled to the Philippines and Central and Eastern Europe with a ministry called International Teams and helped establish Integra Ventures (formerly International Service Centers). This ministry serves owner-operators of small and medium-sized businesses in economically depressed and developing countries.

Near home, Fulton has served on the boards of the YMCA, Day Hospital, and Vision New England. Overseas he has worked with Opportunity International and Integra.

A voracious reader—consuming four or five books at a time—Bob also enjoys playing at golf. "I call myself a gopher, not a golfer. One hits the ball, the other digs holes." He and his wife, Lil, have four daughters and ten grandchildren. When not traveling, they make their home in Framingham, Massachusetts.

Chapter 18
WEB OF LIFE

"Each of us is a better person because of you. We are your symphony.
We are the melody and the notes of your opus and
we are the music of your life."
MR. HOLLAND'S OPUS[1]

Bob Fulton always wanted to be a missionary. Many missionaries stayed in his parents' home, and he expected to follow them overseas when he grew up. A wife and four kids didn't dissuade him. As life unfolded, his geography didn't change, but neither did his zeal to serve God and help others.

Over the years Fulton has affected thousands of lives with his infectious optimism and practical faith—not as a missionary overseas but as the CEO of his own multimillion dollar business based in a Boston suburb. Web Industries, which began in a basement with one machine, has evolved into a holding company with six subsidiaries serving a customer base stretching across the globe.

SECOND CHOICE

Open the Door When Opportunity Knocks

While hustling to pay the bills for his growing family, Fulton had an opportunity to go to work for a company in difficulty. "I figured when it folded I would be free to pursue my interest in missions," Bob says. "Instead the company turned

Entrepreneur: Robert Fulton
Company: Web Industries, Inc.
    Westborough, Massachusetts
Year Started: 1969
Start-up Costs: $10,000
2000 revenues: $30,000,000
Employees: 352

183

around, and I soon found myself running it. When the owner sold it to his son-in-law, I decided to leave because we were on totally different wavelengths."

Direction about what to do next came in the form of a question from his brother. "Why don't you go into business for yourself?" Fulton responded, "I know I'm Irish and I'm handsome, but I'm not rich." It would have ended there, but his father-in-law heard about it. "Being a Scotsman, he had some money and offered me $10,000. I told him I could lose it. He said, 'Nothing ventured, nothing gained.' So I took the $10,000 and started Web Industries. We specialize in converting services: slitting and rewinding of plastic, tape, paper, light-gauge metal—and most anything made in roll form—to customer specs."

Apprentice Yourself to Your Business

Fulton has no M.B.A., not even an undergraduate degree. His business savvy comes from practical experience. "Very few people learn how to do anything in college well enough to make a living at it," says Andy Rooney. "If you want to be an engineer, a scientist, a doctor, or a lawyer, you need a basic education in those specialties, but I've seen a thousand college kids come to work at a job they'd studied and most of them couldn't find their way to the bathroom, let alone help with the work . . . . The way you learn to do a job is to do the job."[2]

Zig Ziglar points out that ten years after college, over 80 percent of graduates earn their living in a field unrelated to their major field of study.[3]

"I don't possess a ton of skills," Bob says. "I'm a risk taker with a bit of the visionary mixed in. I'm not afraid of working hard. I've also had a lot of experience in selling. It fits my personality and temperament well. Yet most of the things necessary to run and grow the business I've had to acquire along the way. I learned the accounting program we put in place as we grew. When computers came along, I figured out the system we needed and picked up some computer skills. I learned it because I had to."

Diversify Your Customer Base

"Initially about 95 percent of our business came from one account—Weyerhaeuser," Fulton recalls, "which later became James River. In 1970 their mill manager called and said they wouldn't be renewing their contract. By June we would be down to virtually no business.

"One of my board members didn't see a problem. 'You've got a plant, equipment, people, money in the bank. Why don't you go and get some business?' We did. By 1971 we had become more diversified. But a few years later when we lost an account comprising 30 percent of our business it again put us in a difficult position, especially since we had just moved into a new building. These trials and difficulties were good for us because they made us trust God. His grace enabled us to survive having had too many eggs in one carton. My advice, if anyone asks, is not to exceed 20 percent of total business with a single customer."

SECOND NATURE

Care Deeply about People

Relationships are the essence of life for Bob Fulton. "I just love people. They are the most important part of our company, more important than productivity. Yet if we care about people, ultimately we benefit from the standpoint of production.

"My passion is mentoring and encouraging folks. We are poor if we don't enjoy relationships. God has made us capable of relating to one another, and ultimately he wants us to have a relationship with him."

Fulton's associates at Web have concluded, "The essence of Bob Fulton is his fascination with people . . . . Your greatest investments have been in people. There was the distraught employee facing a divorce for whom you bought a plane ticket so he could try to reconcile with his wife. There are the young families whom you helped with down payments on their first houses. And there are the many, many people whom you have handed opportunities, pushed to take responsibility, bolstered with constant encouragement—and who achieved more than they dreamed possible."[4]

It's one thing to preach brotherly love, but it's even more powerful to have employees cite—chapter and verse—from the boss's life to prove it.

"In the early stages of the business," Bob remembers, "my primary focus wasn't on the bottom line. I counted it a privilege to stay in business the way I ran it. My reasons for being in business were to provide jobs in an environment that would help people find Christ and grow as Christians. I was more concerned, and still am, with what difference the company will make a hundred years from now."

Did being religious in his approach to business mean Fulton ran a Christian company? "No," he says, "there's no such thing as a Christian company. I did have some Christians working for me, but that didn't make the company Christian."

Lead toward Common Goals

"I believe in a we-can-do-it attitude," asserts Fulton, "and in getting people to work alongside one another to achieve significant goals, not just for the company but also for themselves. You need to provide opportunities for people to grow and feel they are contributing in meaningful ways."

One way Bob has accomplished this is through an employee stock ownership program (ESOP). Transforming employees into owners is good for them and great for customers, as a company brochure explains: "When Web commits to fast, accurate converting services that meet your materials requirements, you are getting the word of the owner. From forklift to slitting equipment to shipping dock—your order is handled by an owner, someone who has staked a part of his or her future on making sure you want to keep doing business with Web."

"The leader is one who mobilizes others toward a goal shared by leader and followers," Garry Wills points out in *Certain Trumpets: the Call of Leadership*. "In that brief definition all three elements are present and are indispensable. Most literature on leadership is unitarian, but life is trinitarian. One legged and two legged chairs do not of themselves stand. A third leg is needed. Leader, followers, and goals make up the three equally necessary supports for leadership.

"Influence is not of itself leadership," Wills continues. "The weather influences us. So do earthquakes or background music in public places. The leader does not just vaguely affect others; he or she takes others toward the object of their joint quest."[5]

Educate Your Workforce

In the article "Books That Transform Companies," *Inc.* magazine highlighted the role of reading at Web. "From the business fable *Zapp!* to DePree's more philosophical *Leadership*, books at Web have provided a floor for companywide debate about everything from internal relationships to what makes for better customer service. Forget the image of the isolated president holed up in his inner sanctum, reading to increase his individual competence. At Web, books are bought in bulk, passed hand to hand, put on meeting agendas, and read out loud.

"'There are two reasons,' says Robert Fulton, Web's founder and president, 'that books may play the major role in the change-of-thinking process going on here.' The first is predictable: books have helped get lots of people thinking about the same concern at the same time. By introducing a book on a carefully chosen subject, Fulton can concentrate his company's attention on areas of trouble or opportunity—teamwork, say, or customer service. The second reason books matter at Web is more subtle. Because it can be so focused and unthreatening, a book-based discussion— it doesn't matter what book is involved—makes it possible for employees at all levels to talk about internal issues they would otherwise never touch."[6]

"I wasn't a very good student," remembers Fulton, "other than the fact I loved to read. I suppose I try to pass that on to other people."

SECOND CHANCE

Take Risks with People

Fulton says, "When I look back, I just chuckle how the whole thing started. I saw the business as a ministry and hired people in difficulty. Most came from hard places, and that created enormous difficulties in running a company profitably. Too often we found ourselves dealing with employee problems rather than customer problems, but we survived and have never lost the vision for helping people."

Web's managers can site a litany of Fulton gambles. "You have never feared to take real risks with people: with the ex-con whom you put in charge of second shift; with the awkward kid whom you assigned significant sales responsibility; with the inexperienced plant manager to whom you entrusted a budget of several million dollars. 'This guy is worth taking a risk on,' we've heard you say over and over."[7]

No place is Fulton's risk-taking more evident than in Web's involvement with ex-convicts. An article on ethics in *U.S. News & World Report* cites Web Industries among "corporations that put people first [and] found that profits followed."

The article includes the story of an ex-con. "'I've worked in places that weren't much different than prison,' recounts Calvin Arey. 'You were pretty much a number.' The 53-year-old Arey, who spent five years behind bars in Massachusetts state prisons, should know. But for six years now, Arey has found a decidedly un-prisonlike atmosphere at Web Industries . . . . Over the course of the past 25 years, Web has employed more than 50 former prisoners, and though they currently make up a fraction of the company's 270-person work force, they symbolize Web's commitment to give people a second chance."[8]

Still, not everyone fits in at Web. "I had to let some people go," Fulton muses. "Never fun, but I was guided by two basic questions: What's best for the person? What's best for the company? Sometimes when I let someone go, it created problems for the company, but if it seemed best for the person to move on, that's what determined my decision."

Nowadays Web's employee-owners participate in the hiring of the people they'll be working with.

Share the Wealth with Those Who Help Make It

"We have always had a profit-sharing program based on a percentage of profits," says Bob. "And when I retired, we set it up so the company would be entirely owned by the employees through a ten-year buyout. Employee stock ownership programs are normally highly leveraged. I didn't want that. I wanted there to be motivation for the company to continue to grow.

"In a unique structure for an ESOP, I pegged the stock at $250 a share at the beginning, and it will remain the same for the whole ten years. I sell a certain number of shares each year to the company at this fixed price. The goal is to see the price double, so the employees pay $250 a share for stock worth $500. They pick up the value created by their labor. I consider this a win-win arrangement. So far things have gone well."

Web's treatment of its employee-owners has been so exemplary that even Congress has taken notice. "In a vivid display of the employee owner coming to Washington," according to *The ESOP Report*, "Rob Zicaro, a machine operator at Web Industries in Framingham, Massachusetts, testified before the Senate Committee on Labor and Human Resources on how employee ownership can lead to a more competitive U.S. workforce.

"Zicaro, named New England Employee Owner of the Year by the ESOP Association, told senators, 'I work on the factory floor and I'm a stockholder in my company. In the near future, we will be 100 percent employee-owned. And at 40 years old, to own part of a company, to own a piece of the rock, is the American dream.'"[9]

The machinist has also spoken to President Clinton and other leaders on what's going on at Web, named the ESOP Association's 1993 Company of the Year. "It's not so much the ownership of stock or how much is in my account—although that's important," says one Web employee-owner, "it's that somebody believes in me."

SECOND CHILDHOOD

Lighten Up, You'll Live Longer

In a letter to "Fulty" on the twentieth anniversary of Web's founding, the management team expressed their appreciation for Fulton's zest for life. While acknowledging he could be a "tough and demanding boss, seldom satisfied when something is finished—it can always be built upon or improved," they also praised his lighter side. "Throughout the years your energy and exuberance have always amazed us. Whatever you do, you do with all your heart. And you seem to enjoy every minute . . . . No one has more fun than Fulty! And nobody crams more life into each day!"

Power doesn't require pretentiousness. One of this century's most influential holy men, Angelo Giuseppi Roncalli—better known as Pope John XXIII—knew this. "I always try to show people that I am a regular person. I have two eyes, a nose—a very big one—a mouth, two ears, and so on."

He wrote in his journal when he felt overwhelmed by the responsibilities of the papacy, "Giovanni, don't take yourself that seriously!"[10]

Enjoy Retirement when the Time Comes

Bob initially thought he would be out of Web by age fifty-five. "I overshot that and didn't retire until sixty. People said to me, 'How can you leave your baby?' It's hard to let go, but I think God has something else for me to do, and I'm excited about it.

"Since then I've devoted more time to my interest in missions. Like a kid in a candy shop, I put my hands into everything and quickly landed on ten boards. It soon became painfully obvious I couldn't do everything and do it well, so I've cut back. For the first three or four years of retirement I spent half of each year traveling. My wife tries to get me to slow down, but I enjoy enormously the people I'm meeting and the work I'm doing here and abroad.

"I get up every day thrilled about the opportunities I have to build relationships. The company kept me pretty well hemmed in day to day. Now I'm freer to pursue my passion to mentor and encourage young people, primarily in the marketplace. I'm having a ball!"

SUMMARY OF KEY PRINCIPLES

- Open the door when opportunity knocks.
- Apprentice yourself to your business.
- Diversify your customer base.
- Care deeply about people.
- Lead toward common goals.
- Educate your workforce.
- Take risks with people.
- Share the wealth with those who help make it.
- Lighten up, you'll live longer.
- Enjoy retirement when the time comes.

INFLUENTIAL BOOKS—
RECOMMENDED READING

Byham, William C., with Jeff Cox. *Zapp! The Lightning of Empowerment.* New York: Fawcett Books, 1988.

Carlzon, Jan. *Moment of Truth.* New York: Harper & Row, 1989.

Schein, Edgar H. *Organizational Culture and Leadership.* San Francisco: Jossey-Bass, 1985.

Senge, Peter M. *The Fifth Discipline: The Art and Practice of the Learning Organization.* New York: Doubleday, 1990.

KEN DAHLBERG spent his early years on a farm in Wisconsin. "In today's world we would be regarded as poor," he remembers. As a teenager he moved to St. Paul to finish high school. He worked at the Lowery Hotel, and by the time he got drafted in 1941, he was the catering manager for the Pick Hotels in Chicago.

After completing officer's training school, Ken became a flight instructor until being sent to Europe before D-Day. He came home with a chest full of medals, including fifteen air medals, two Purple Hearts, a Silver Star, two Distinguished Flying Crosses, and the Distinguished Service Cross (second only to the Congressional Medal of Honor).

Dahlberg has been active in local and national politics throughout his life, being introduced to the Republican Party through his flying buddy, Barry Goldwater. For twenty-seven years he served on various college and university boards, including the Air Force Academy.

Bausch & Lomb purchased Dahlberg, Inc., in 1993. Ken remains active in business through his own venture capital firm. He enjoys golf, fishing, hunting, and reading. He's been married to Betty Jayne over half a century. They have three children and live in Deephaven, Minnesota.

Chapter 19
WHERE'S THE ACTION?

"Trust yourself: You know more than you think."
BENJAMIN SPOCK, M.D.[1]

Ken Dahlberg craves action. During his tour of duty over Europe in World War II, he became one of only a handful of "triple aces" by downing fifteen enemy aircraft. Shot down himself three times, he ended the war in a POW camp after two failed escape attempts.

"It wasn't fun (being a POW)," Dahlberg relates in the book *Top Guns*, "but it was tolerable and I learned a lot in that short time. I learned how to get along better with other people under duress. I learned to appreciate small things like a shower once a week, or once a month, and a piece of bad dark bread (partly sawdust) three times a day and a wormy cabbage soup once a week."[2]

Returning Stateside after the war, his resourcefulness landed him a job with the Telex Company. Three years later he launched Dahlberg, Inc., a business that would grow to $100 million in annual revenues by the time he sold it in 1993.

TAKING OFF

Bet on Your Skills

"While at Telex I started a new division," Ken recalls, "the electro-acoustics division. At the time I was helping reactivate the Minnesota Air National Guard and flying P-51s on weekends. We used

Entrepreneur: Ken Dahlberg
Company: Dahlberg, Inc.
(d/b/a Miracle-Ear)
Golden Valley, Minnesota
Year Started: 1948
Start-up Costs: $1,000
1993 Revenues: $100,000,000
(when company was sold)
Employees: 500

these old-fashioned headsets, and I looked at these little hearing aid parts and figured I could make a better unit. I designed one and got Telex into the headset business. Today, over fifty years later, Telex is still the premier headset maker.

"In 1948 I decided to go on my own. Like many farm kids I thought I could do it better myself. As my dad always said, 'Farmers know where the handle is.' With the thousand-dollar salary that had accumulated while a POW, I set up Dahlberg, Inc. I hired an engineer, not being one myself. I had concepts but lacked the electrical engineering background to create the products. I told him what I wanted and let him figure out how to make it."

Why trade a good job with an established company for a high-risk start-up? You would as well ask Dahlberg why he strapped an airplane to his backside and bet his life on his skills in a dogfight. "I suppose it's my sense that I could do it better than somebody else. That's what I felt at that age. After being a fighter pilot, life seemed slow most of the time. I constantly looked for action."

"Scholars have discerned among leaders an inclination from early childhood for risk taking and a willingness to go to great lengths—often in defiance of others, including those in positions of authority—in order to achieve their ends," says Harvard professor Howard Gardner. "A motive to gain power—either for its own sake or in pursuit of a specific aim—is invariably present. This capacity to take risks speaks to a confidence that one will at least sometimes attain success; implacability in the face of opposition likewise reflects a willingness to rely on oneself and not to succumb to others' strictures and reservations."[3]

Innovate to Meet Basic Human Needs

What pushed Ken to break formation and go solo was his invention of the "pillow radio," a device allowing hospital patients to listen to the radio without clumsy headsets. When Telex refused to develop the idea, Dahlberg pursued the opportunity by starting his own company. Nurse call systems, patient monitoring systems, and other hospital communication devices followed. Soon he started manufacturing hearing aids. "We branched into two divisions and both prospered," he recalls.

In what became known as the Dahlberg Creed, Ken wrote out his mission: "To help every person suffering from man's oldest incurable disease, that silent, painless destroyer of human communication . . . deafness . . . rendering this service with dignity and devotion to client and community." This became my *raison d'être*. "As an aside," Dahlberg includes, "you should have your purpose for being in writing. Anything you can't define in writing isn't worth trying to do."

Beerbohm's First Law, coined by essayist Sir Max Beerbohm, says, "Anything that is worth doing has been done frequently. Things hitherto undone should be given, I suspect, a wide berth."[4] Dahlberg disagrees.

"The challenge of designing a better hearing aid particularly intrigued Dahlberg," reports the *Saint Paul Pioneer Press*. "Hearing aids in those days were bulky and unsightly, with a separate microphone unit typically attached to an earpiece by a cord. Dahlberg wanted to create a virtually invisible hearing aid, and someone said if he could do that, 'it would be a miracle.'"[5] In 1955 Dahlberg debuted the world's first all-in-the-ear hearing aid, appropriately named Miracle-Ear.

The introduction of the first electronic hearing aid worn in the ear proved only the beginning. "We kept our focus on benefits to our users," Ken recounts. "In our lab we had a sign in big, bold letters: 'What is the user benefit of the product you're working on?'" More innovations followed the original Miracle-Ear:

1957—Magic-Earrings, cosmetically concealed Magic-Ear II receivers.

1959—Solar Ear, the first solar-powered hearing aid.

1962—Miracle-Ear IV, the first hearing aid with integrated circuitry.

Quality wasn't sacrificed at the shrine of inventiveness. In 1957 the company earned the coveted Good Housekeeping Seal of Approval.

GAINING ALTITUDE

Stay Open to Timely Opportunities

Ken didn't hesitate to strike out on his own and put his name and resources on the line. Nor was he reluctant to give up that independence when it made good business sense. "In the late 1950s I joined YPO (Young Presidents Organization,)," says Dahlberg. "There I met Bob

Gavin, president of Motorola. We became good friends. He liked our people and product ideas, and he bought our company in 1959. For five years we were a wholly owned subsidiary of Motorola."

The resources now available to Dahlberg, Inc., accelerated new product development, which resulted in the smallest and lightest hearing aids on the market, distributed nationwide through 250 locations. Business prospered, but gravitational forces would soon alter the corporate landscape. "In 1964 Motorola decided to divest itself of all consumer products," says Ken. "By this time I knew I wasn't interested in being a big corporation guy. Using the leverage of my Motorola stock, I borrowed the money to buy back the hearing aid division."

Change is the dealer in the game of life. Successful business people, like good gamblers, look at what they've been dealt and instinctively know, according to Kenny Rogers, "when to hold 'em, when to fold 'em, when to walk away, and when to run." Raising the ante, Dahlberg once more held the Miracle-Ear card, and by the time the next corporate high roller came along to buy it, it would have a face value of $139 million.

But that would be thirty years in the future.

Use High Tech to Maintain High Touch

"When I bought the division from Motorola," Dahlberg says, "we were doing about $5 million in business. By 1982 we were doing about $13 million. After deregulation we shot up to $100 million by 1993. We did this primarily by reestablishing our franchise system. This gave better distribution and led to greater profits, which meant more money for research and development and resulted in better products.

"We became well known for our franchise distribution system. It enabled us to give superior customer service. Convenience rings cash registers. We had a thousand stores in the United States and another hundred stores overseas. These locations were uniform in appearance, and our personnel were uniformly trained. We had standardized testing equipment, and our stores were linked by computers. We were among the first companies to use technology to provide unvarying service. No matter where you went across the country, when you entered a Miracle-Ear office, you felt at home, and the people there had immediate access to your records."

Miracle-Ear created the first franchising agreements in the industry. The company also secured the concession rights to Sears' hearing aid centers and in 1989 established a similar partnership with Montgomery Ward. These strategic alliances illustrate Dahlberg's belief in the importance of teamwork.

FLYING IN FORMATION

Do It Yourself, but Not by Yourself

Dahlberg's military training has shaped his approach to life and business. "I had a fabulous military experience, which taught me two important lessons. They don't sound inclusive, but they are. First, the army taught me how to take care of myself. Second, take care of your buddy, and your buddy will take care of you. In combat you know you won't be left behind. If they have to drag you out dead, they will. That sense of teamwork is a great feeling.

"Teamwork is about delegation and trust," Ken continues. "In business you start with an idea, then you transmit your vision and get others caught up in it. If the vision is clear, this isn't difficult. Next you have to trust people to carry out your vision because your own radius of action is only about as long as your arm.

"When we hired people for the assembly line, we paid good money for their fingers and got their brains for free. When we woke up to the fact that their brains were more important than their fingers, it helped us bring out the best in people. Everyone benefited."

The most important teams in Ken's life these days are neither military nor corporate, but spiritual. "The Friday morning men's renewal group and the Bible Study Fellowship group of which I am a member continue to have a profound effect on my life," says Ken. "Both began at the Central Lutheran Church where I have been a member since 1945."

Surround Yourself with Experience

Back to business. In addition to an inside team, Dahlberg stresses the need for outside experts. Nicholas Butler defines an expert as "someone who knows more and more about less and less."[6] "You can't be a successful entrepreneur today," Dalhberg maintains, "unless you surround yourself with a good lawyer, a good finance person, and a good banker. They'll see to it you get a good team assembled: engineering, production, marketing— whatever you need. Business is so specialized today you need experts in every facet. It's different from fifty years ago."

Ditto from Harvey Mackay, who writes in *Swim with the Sharks*, "When I first bought Mackay envelope, I was 25. My lawyer—the one I hired after I fired the young hotshot who told me not to buy the envelope company— was 60. My accountant was 58, and my banker would admit to being 70, but I think he was closer to 80. They didn't know a thing about the envelope business, but they didn't need to. They had seen enough business problems in their lifetimes to be able to deal with anything imaginable without knowing the ins and outs of my particular industry. And although everything that happened to me in my first five years of business was new to me, nothing was new to them."[7]

SETTING YOUR COMPASS

Order Your Priorities around Personal Faith

"I grew up in a good Christian family, and I had the advantage of that background," says Dalhberg, "My mom and dad exemplified common sense, integrity, and industry, and my wonderful wife, Betty Jayne, has the same virtues. They helped shape a personal philosophy that's served me well. I try to put God first, family second, country third, and business fourth. And yet, all of these are intertwined; getting them out of balance will always cause pain."

While Ken got his philosophy from his parents, he couldn't inherit their faith. "Initially my perception of the whole religious scene may be compared to a still picture," he recalls. "I thanked God for good fortune, asked him for favors, read the Bible stories as beautiful poetry and—as a world traveler—wondered about the claims of several world religions as being the real thing. But through the impact of Christians who came into my life, my still picture came alive!

"One Catholic priest in particular helped me realize I was carrying an unnecessary burden of guilt. He pointed to a crucifix on the wall and invited me to 'come down off the cross,' telling me there was only room for one there. Jesus had died on the cross for my sins. Wow! This was a simple description of God's grace I could understand and grasp. Now he was alive and the helper he sent to earth after his resurrection, the Holy Spirit, activated my consciousness. I believed and entered a new life that has been more meaningful, joyful, and easier."

What about the impact of putting business fourth? "I think it helped us at Miracle-Ear," Dahlberg reflects, "because there's a certain moral order to things. If your business plan lines up with that order, good things happen; at least they have for me. Having your priorities in order makes it easier to get good people and good people tend to stick around, which is good for the company. When you get to number four—the business—then the customer is number one. Business is as simple as finding and fulfilling human needs in a seamless process."

This commitment to customer service and product support—as evidenced by the Miracle-Ear Hearing Care Guarantee—has made Miracle-Ear one of the most recognized and trusted names in hearing aids.

Decide to Do Good as Part of Doing Business

Before written mission statements became popular, Miracle-Ear had the Dahlberg Creed. "A creed is nothing more than a set of objectives," explains the company's founder. "An objective is a never-ending pursuit, as opposed to a goal, which is more finite and only a part of the objective. Our creed spelled out our desire to help people suffering from deafness."

Helping the hearing-impaired is the center but not the circumference of Dahlberg's concern for others. In 1990 the company established the Miracle-Ear Children's Foundation. "We had policies expressing our values. Three percent of our profits went to charity. If any of our employees wanted to go to school, we would pay for it. We hired people others might not have hired."

This last form of benevolence came about through less-than-altruistic motives, Dahlberg candidly admits. "We had several hundred Southeast Asians in our assembly plant in Minneapolis. Hiring them wasn't something I initially intended to do. One day in church the minister came up to me and said, 'I've got a couple of Asians who need jobs.' I didn't want to hire them, but I couldn't turn down the minister, so I hired these two Vietnamese people. They turned out to be charming and wonderful young people. We wound up with three hundred Southeast Asians working for us. What a blessing they became to our company!"

Keep Dreaming, but Stay Awake

"You have to keep dreaming as an entrepreneur," Dahlberg believes, "but you also have to listen for alarms to wake you up occasionally. When your ambitions get ahead of your resources and you run out of money, the alarm bells should go off."

Then what do you do? "Well," says Dahlberg, "you may want to take your company public, especially if it's a cash-intensive business. That's what I did. My unusually competent brother, Arnold, and I owned it all when Motorola purchased Dahlberg, Inc. After we bought it back, we eventually went public. In 1993 when we sold it, I owned about 40 percent."

A willingness to follow your dreams and a shrewd sense of timing are critical to business success, but so, believes Dahlberg, is divine intervention. Flashback to February 28, 1945. "I was leading our squadron of eight Thunderbolts home from a successful dive-bombing and strafing mission. We had climbed to ten thousand feet, and I had just received a radio check from the flight leaders behind me, advising that we were crossing friendly lines. The report was interrupted by puffs of ugly 88mm flak. The next thing I knew, I was less than five hundred feet from the ground in a just-opened chute. It seemed incredible that I could be blown free, not only from the plane, but the seat-belt harness as well, free-fall unconscious through 9,500 feet, then regain consciousness in split-second time to pull the rip cord (by rote, I have no memory of it). The landing was very hard, but I was safe." Small wonder the chapter in *Top Guns* where he relates this story concludes with Dahlberg's hearty "Praise the Lord!

"Why did God provide a safety net for me during this and, indeed, all the harrowing experiences of my life?" Ken asks, looking back over the intervening half century. "I am certain he had his loving arm around me for a purpose, saving me for another day and another mission that I am only now beginning to fulfill."

In the air and on the ground, Ken Dahlberg's life displays honed skill and humble dependence, the aplomb of an ace and the confidence of a child. Looking back, is there anything he would do differently other than avoid getting shot down so often? "There is one other thing," he muses. "I would go fishing more."[8]

SUMMARY OF KEY PRINCIPLES

- Bet on your skills.
- Innovate to meet basic human needs.
- Stay open to timely opportunities.
- Use high tech to maintain high touch.
- Do it yourself, but not by yourself.
- Surround yourself with experience.
- Order your priorities around personal faith.
- Decide to do good as part of doing business.
- Keep dreaming, but stay awake.

INFLUENTIAL BOOKS— RECOMMENDED READING

Bork, Robert. *Slouching Toward Gomorrah.* New York: HarperCollins, 1997.

Grisham, John. *The Partner.* New York: Doubleday, 1997.

Packer, J. I. *Knowing God.* Downers Grove, Ill.: InterVarsity Press, 1973.

Stanley, Thomas J., and William D. Danko. *The Millionaire Next Door.* Atlanta: Longstreet Press, 1996.

DAVID V. CAVAN is president of Cavan Real Estate Investments, a development company located in Scottsdale, Arizona. He has more than twenty years of experience in real estate management, development, investments, and brokerage.

Dave started Cavan Associates in 1976 as a commercial brokerage operation and later refined its focus to include residential and commercial developments. He has developed more than three million square feet of commercial office and retail space together with numerous subdivisions, with a total project value in excess of half a billion dollars. These projects are located in Arizona, New Mexico, California, and Nebraska.

After graduating from military school at Booneville, Missouri, Cavan attended Bradley University in Peoria, Illinois, and Marquette University in Milwaukee. He is a faithful member of Scottsdale Bible Church and serves on the boards of various Christian and humanitarian organizations. He has also assisted in fund-raising activities for various Christian groups like Campus Crusade for Christ, and Mission of Mercy.

Dave's passions include golf, bird hunting, and riding his Harley with his friends. His *best* friend is Karen, his wife of almost forty years. The Cavans have four children and seven grandchildren and live in Scottsdale, Arizona.

Chapter 20

BACK FROM THE BRINK

"If things go wrong, do not go with them."
ROGER W. BABSON[1]

This chapter is not about starting a business but about saving one. This is an important skill for entrepreneurs because of the high failure rate of business start-ups. Eighty percent of them fail in the first five years, according to consultant Michael Gerber. "And the rest of the bad news is, if you own a small business that has managed to survive for five years or more, don't breathe a sigh of relief. Because more than eighty percent of the small businesses that survive the first five years fail in the second five."[2]

In 1988, 63,853 businesses filed for bankruptcy according to the American Bankruptcy Institute.[3] Dave Cavan was not among them, though by all rights he should have been.

EXPLOSION!

Expect Some Explosions in the Minefield of Life

The roots of Cavan Investments can be traced back to 1970. Incorporated in 1976, the company had its best year ever in 1986. With more than two hundred million dollars in properties under management and offices in three states, Cavan enjoyed the respect of his peers and all the toys that come with success.

Entrepreneur: David Cavan
Company: Cavan Real Estate
   Investments
   Scottsdale, Arizona
Year Started: 1976
Start-up Costs: $2,500
1999 Revenues: $40,000,000
Employees: 28

His prosperity came as a result of hard work and shrewd investing, but life wasn't all business. "I always tried to be a good husband and dad," reflects this father of four. "I supported many Christian organizations and served on several boards. God had blessed my company, and I talked about how he owned it and I just managed it. Still, despite this outward success, I felt an emptiness inside—something I couldn't get rid of. I was bored. At one point I even started negotiations to sell the business."

Then the bomb went off, and Cavan Investments started to sink in 1987. "I had a number of large projects either under construction or in the process of being leased up," Dave says, "but I couldn't find tenants. Loans came due, and I couldn't pay them. The financial pressures mounted.

"Most of us sail through life learning to adjust and adapt," Cavan continues. "But every once in a while a bomb goes off and changes everything. It could be a death in the family, a health problem, something with our children, or a financial crisis. Whatever it is, it just blows us away. We don't choose these bombs, but we get to choose how we will respond to them."

Refuse to Become a Victim

Dave is convinced that bombs go off for a reason, and we have to resist the temptation to become victims when they do. "Don't ask 'why' questions," he cautions. "'Why' questions are the questions of a victim: 'Why did they do this to me? Why did that happen?' Instead, ask 'how' questions: 'How can I learn from this? How can I help others through this?'

"I resisted the temptation to go looking for excuses. I knew I could blame my problem on the decline in the real estate market or the change in the tax laws or even the Savings and Loan crisis—very fashionable at the time. However, if I blamed circumstances, I might miss what God was trying to teach me. And if I didn't learn what I needed to know, God would get my attention some other time, some other way."

Charles Swindoll, president of Dallas Theological Seminary, underscores the importance of choosing to respond positively to adversity. "The remarkable thing is we have a choice every day regarding the attitude we will embrace from that day. We cannot change our past; we cannot change the fact that people will act in a certain way. We cannot change the inevitable. The only thing that we can do is play on the one string that we have and this string is, attitude. I am convinced that life is ten percent what happens to me and ninety percent how I react to it. And so it is with you . . . . We are in charge of our attitudes."[4]

"I decided to be a learner, not a victim," says Dave with conviction. "I clung to God's promise in Philippians 4:13, 'I can do all things through Christ who strengthens me.' I had an inner peace. Still, the future frightened me. I owed $160 million that I was personally guaranteed on."

TRIAGE

Do All You Can and Trust God for the Rest

"When things started to disintegrate, I became more hands-on and tried to fix the problems," Cavan recalls. "I cut my executive staff and took back responsibilities I had once delegated. I worked harder than ever before in my life. I believed that somehow I could pull this out. The emphasis was on *me*. I could do it."

However, business kept eroding, and Dave's self-confidence dissolved along with it. "Eventually I realized I couldn't make it work by myself. I knew God could lease up my buildings; yet he wasn't doing that. The market was bad, but we had been through bad markets before. What was different now? My world was crumbling, and for the first time in my career, I faced something I couldn't fix."

It was also something from which Dave couldn't hide.

"It's embarrassing when others see us in difficulty. Our tendency is to hide when we're hurting. Don't do it," Cavan warns with the voice of experience. "You need to share your feelings, to be open and honest with those you can trust. You need family and friends to help you maintain perspective when you're going through troubles.

"I decided to be real. No more pretending. I was going broke. No more big developer image. I would be honest and let the chips fall where they may. I knew I could keep fighting, keep working harder, borrow more money, or I could file for bankruptcy. I had three reasons for not wanting to go the bankruptcy route. First, I thought it would be more honoring to God if I could get through this without using the courts. Second, I didn't want to put my wife, Karen, through the public pain of bankruptcy.

Finally, I had two sons in the real estate business, and I felt it would be better for them if their dad didn't go bankrupt."

Get the Best Advice, Then Follow Your Heart

"Bankruptcy is a form of grace, and there is a place for it," Dave believes, "but I decided to avoid it if I could. I interviewed the best bankruptcy attorneys in town, and they all said the same thing: 'We can stretch this out for years. You can get a nice salary during this time and probably come out of it with a building or two.' They made it sound so easy.

"Next, I retained the attorney I felt was the best of the bunch and told him his job was to keep me out of bankruptcy. He thought I was crazy and told me I'd spend a lot of money and still end up having to file. In October 1988, against his advice, I arranged a meeting with all my bankers. There were seven of them. I got them in a room and made a proposal to each, giving copies of the proposals to all the others. Everything was on the table, and everybody knew what everybody else's deal was.

"I explained in detail my current financial situation and my desire to work things out. Six of the banks went together with my proposal. One did not. In order for the deal to work, it had to be unanimous. I now realized that everything I'd worked for over the last seventeen years would be lost.

"The next five months were tough," Dave says. "By February 1989, I had sold several properties and given all the proceeds to the bank. The ones I couldn't sell I deeded back. I took the balance of my assets—including our house—and put them into a trust for the benefit of the banks. Finally, I signed a deficiency note to the banks for three million dollars, due in three years."

RECOVERY

Focus on What Really Matters in Life

During these difficult times, Dave learned the wisdom of the bumper sticker that says, "It's not hard to meet expenses—they're everywhere!" Assets, on the other hand, were as scarce as snow in Scottsdale. "I owed three million dollars," says the one-time millionaire. "I questioned my abilities. How would I support myself? How would I pay back this loan? Where was my identity? Should I get out of the real estate business? Should we move to another state?

"I would drive by the buildings I used to own and a feeling of sadness would come over me. Some days I didn't want to get out of bed. I had bouts of depression, and when I went to work, I didn't know what to do.

"To refocus my mind I started reading the old Christian classics—books by Murray, Finney, Bounds, and other writers of faith. I put Bible verses on 3" x 5" cards and repeated them over and over throughout the day. I saturated myself with God's Word and drew renewed strength from it.

"In March we moved from our large house on a golf course to a rented condo in McCormick Ranch," recalls Cavan. "We sold everything we had—cars, land, oceanfront condos. The only thing I didn't sell was Karen's jewelry, which I'd given her over the last twenty-eight years. A few months later our condo was robbed and the jewelry taken. Of course, it wasn't insured.

"I have been blessed with a wonderful family and lots of close friends who went through this ordeal with me," Cavan adds. "They gave counsel and support. But my number one counselor was Karen. When I told her we were going to lose the house in which we'd raised our four children, she said, 'Well, it's too big anyway now that the kids are gone. It's time to move.' Watching her, I realized that things aren't important, relationships are. She had her priorities in order. When everything was gone, rather than complain, she told me she felt relieved that we no longer had all that pressure. For years I used being able to buy nice things for my family as an excuse for overworking. Now I was learning that all my family really wanted was just more of me—the same thing God wanted."

Let Trials Drive You toward God, Not Away from Him

"I have the gift of giving," Dave says about himself. "Early in my career I sometimes even borrowed money to give it away when I saw a need I wanted to meet. As my income grew, so did my giving, but the percentage became less. I kept more and more of what I earned. Looking back now, I realize that my possessions were possessing me. I didn't plan it that way; it just happened. The deceit of riches is very subtle.

"About this time, a close friend pointed out to me that I was a hoarder. I had no idea what a hoarder was, so I looked it up. As I thought about it I saw he was right. I would buy and keep things, even if I didn't need them.

'If things get tough,' I told myself, 'I'll have this to fall back on.' I was trusting in my things rather than God. I had so much stuff that I didn't need God. Well, he fixed that.

"'No discipline seems pleasant at the time, but painful,'" Cavan quotes from Hebrews 12:11. "'Later on, however, it produces a harvest of righteousness and peace for those who have been trained by it.'"

W. P. Purkiser says it another way. "God helps us to do what we can and endure what we must, even in the darkest hour. But more, He wants to teach us there are no rainbows without storm clouds and there are no diamonds without heavy pressure and enormous heat."[5]

It wasn't an easy season for Cavan, but the clouds eventually lifted and the pot at the end of his rainbow is no longer empty. "God has blessed me in so many ways in the last ten years," says Dave. "I was able to stay in the real estate business and do consulting work for the banks. I took over and managed some of their properties: recasting them, filling them up, or selling them. I earned commissions for my work.

"I also started doing some lot development. Through the income generated from those developments, I was able to pay off my loans by August 1993, just a little over three years from the time I signed them. Cavan Investments is once again developing office buildings."

ADVICE

Help Others with What You've Learned

Today Cavan has a great relationship with the banks, though he seldom needs to use them anymore. "Instead of borrowing the funds needed," he says, "I now have a group of 125 investors that partner with me on a regular basis. Our projects are substantially oversubscribed by these investors."

On several occasions Dave has had the chance to tell his story and to pass along some advice about surviving the landmines of life. He has six pieces of hard-earned advice for those in need of triage.

1. *Pray.* Seek the Lord. Focus on him, not your problems. Look up, not in.

2. *Seek counsel.* Don't isolate yourself. You need others to help you make it through tough times.

3. *Take care of yourself.* Get enough rest and relaxation. Exercise. Eat healthy.
4. *Focus on tomorrow.* Don't hang on to the past. Look to the future.
5. *Develop a plan.* Access your situation. Access your abilities. Don't be stagnant.
6. *Make a decision.* Once you decide what you're going to do, do it!

"To me it's unthinkable to go through life without a personal relationship with Jesus Christ," concludes this reborn businessman. "He has a purpose for everything he allows to happen to us, including the bombs. When they go off in our lives—and they will—we can lean on the God who loves us.

"'Cast all your cares on him because he cares for you,'" quotes Cavan from 1 Peter 5:7. The text goes on to promise that 'the God of all grace, who called you to his eternal glory in Christ, after you have suffered a little while, will himself restore you and make you strong, firm, and steadfast.'"

As Dave will attest, this promise is bombproof.

SUMMARY OF KEY PRINCIPLES

- Expect some explosions in the minefield of life.
- Refuse to become a victim.
- Do all you can and trust God for the rest.
- Get the best advice, then follow your heart.
- Focus on what really matters in life.
- Let trials drive you toward God, not away from him.
- Help others with what you've learned.

INFLUENTIAL BOOKS— RECOMMENDED READING

Blackaby, Henry, and Claude V. King. *Experiencing God: Knowing and Doing His Will.* Nashville: Broadman & Holman, 1998.

Boreham, F. W. *The Prodigal.* (out of print)

Chambers, Oswald. *My Utmost for His Highest.* Grand Rapids: Discovery House, 1992.

Taylor, Dr. and Mrs. Howard. *Hudson Taylor's Spiritual Secret.* Chicago: Moody Press, 1987.

SUMMARY OF KEY PRINCIPLES

1. FOSTER FRIESS

- Earn trust by giving it.
- Take responsibility for your actions.
- Get the facts before making decisions.
- Go the extra mile.
- Prioritize for productivity.
- Monitor your proficiency.
- Avoid meetings whenever possible.
- Put first things first and last things not at all.
- Develop team spirit through serving others.
- Accentuate the positive.

2. BOB BUFORD

- Center your life around specific goals.
- Ask the right questions of success.
- Move beyond success to significance.
- Create and invest social capital.
- Work only on things that will make a big difference if you succeed.
- Devote yourself to lifelong learning.
- Write your own epitaph.
- Discover and follow your calling.
- Concentrate on what you do well.

3. NOEL IRWIN HENTSCHEL

- Say yes to yourself when others say no.
- View your market from a different perspective.
- Build on strategic partnerships.
- Expand through win-win relationships.
- Think ahead of the competition.
- Refuse to take "UN" for an answer.
- Be wary of consultants.
- Accept the responsibilities of success.
- Leverage your strengths to benefit the weak.
- Balance family, faith, business, and community.

4. JERRY COLANGELO

- Build a community, not an empire.
- Trust God's plan for you.
- Envision the future you want to create.
- Embrace the responsibility of being a role model.
- Foster consensus to improve competitiveness.
- Invest in good character.
- Pay people what they're worth.
- Promote your values with your wealth.
- Protect home base.
- Stay in the game as long as you love it.

5. W. ROBERT STOVER

- Run with a concept that's ahead of its time.
- Solve the cash flow problems that come with growth.
- Bank on your principles.
- Treat employees like family.
- Focus on creating value and let success take care of itself.
- Make positive values a forethought, not an afterthought.
- Know when to get rid of Santa.
- Have a realistic time frame for your dreams.
- Pass the baton smoothly.

6. HERMAN CAIN

- Open doors by exceeding expectations.
- Have a risk index "north of .5."
- Start over if necessary to climb higher.
- Identify and remove barriers to growth.
- Block out the unnecessary.
- Get ugly to get results.
- Partner with people you trust.
- Believe in yourself and others.
- Give God the glory.

7. NORMAN MILLER

- Conquer your personal demons.
- Include spirituality in the workplace.
- Seek divine guidance.
- Pay attention to promotion and packaging.
- Consolidate around prime strengths.
- Excel at helping others excel.
- Crank it up 15 percent, but don't electrocute yourself.
- Reallocate your time to pursue your passions.
- Relish playing on the house's money.

8. JOHN BRADLEY

- Convert insight into income.
- Grow by trial and error.
- Give away razors to sell blades.
- Maximize your God-given talents.
- Strive for a 60-40 balance at work.
- Initiate, develop, or die.
- Engender loyalty that overcomes incompetence.
- Attract creative problem solvers.
- Make benefits a sticking point.
- Listen to inside experts.
- Calibrate the human factors as you grow.
- Have a knack for what you do.

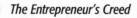

9. ROSEMARY JORDANO

- Use your head to follow your heart.
- Find a way around roadblocks.
- Pull the trigger when passion and profit line up.
- Prepare your supply lines in advance.
- Document the need for your services.
- Specialize in win-win solutions.
- Set the standard for excellence in your field.
- Enrich the communities where you do business.
- Deploy a safety net between you and the ground.
- Leave an indelible impact on those you serve.

10. JAMES H. AMOS JR.

- Commit to a concept with a future.
- Don't reinvent the wheel.
- Lower your risk with a Business Format Franchise.
- Raise your chance of success by getting branded.
- Concentrate on maintaining good relationships.
- Instill moral values into your business.
- Team up with trusted partners to offer better services.
- Practice forgiveness as a way of life.
- See yourself as working for your father's company.

11. JEFFREY MCKEEVER

- Turn disappointments into discoveries.
- Act today on what you expect to happen tomorrow.
- Mortgage the present to build the future.
- Beware of means that blur the end.
- Redefine yourself around a stable core.
- Lead from your values.
- Maintain the tension between control and growth.
- Service what you sell.
- Take care of *all* your stakeholders.
- Be unreasonable about progress.

12. THE CATHYS

- Pour a solid foundation of hard work.
- Find the right place for your business concept to blossom.
- Insist on superior quality in your signature products.
- Strive to satisfy every customer.
- Be a faithful steward of your people resources.
- Reward good management.
- Preserve the core; push the edge.
- Find your weaknesses and fix them, *ad nauseam.*
- Help those who can't help themselves.
- Cultivate new shoots from old roots.
- Bring your faith to work.

13. CHRISTOPHER CRANE

- Know if and when to buy.
- Pray as part of planning . . . but not in place of planning.
- Determine if an IPO is right for you.
- Do it right if you go public.
- Don't let cash make you dumb.
- Develop an Internet strategy.
- Recruit only AA players for your team.
- Set the example in caring for others.
- Acknowledge divine providence.

14. MICHAEL MANSON

- Live with passion!
- Seek the truth, the whole truth, and nothing but the truth.
- Speak the truth in love.
- Honor those in authority.
- Start over if necessary.
- Let the leaders set the pace.
- Make transitions with integrity.
- Face life with boldness and courage.
- Trust God and others with your life.

15. ESTEAN LENYOUN

- Pursue your dreams while learning your trade.
- See diamonds where others see coal.
- Put God in his place and he will put you in yours.
- Treat your background as an asset instead of a liability.
- Consider crossing over to the social sector.
- Harmonize a ministry heart with a business mind.
- Equip others to succeed.
- Go after the mentors you need.

16. KIRK HUMPHREYS

- Escape the complacency that can come with success.
- Make life transitions with care.
- Pursue fresh challenges outside of business.
- Follow your sense of calling, even to unexpected places.
- Give your time and talents to causes you believe in.
- Live for something bigger than yourself.
- Ensure future freedom through hard work.
- Dare to be a Daniel.

17. JACQUELINE BACA

- Work your way into leadership, even if your name is on the door.
- Put yourself on the line for your ideas.
- Build on strengths where family is involved.
- School yourself for the benefit of others.
- Improve people's lives as part of your mission.
- Expand production capacity without compromising product quality.
- Protect the environment as standard operating procedure.
- Assume others want to do the right thing.

18. ROBERT FULTON

- Open the door when opportunity knocks.
- Apprentice yourself to your business.
- Diversify your customer base.

- Care deeply about people.
- Lead toward common goals.
- Educate your workforce.
- Take risks with people.
- Share the wealth with those who help make it.
- Lighten up, you'll live longer.
- Enjoy retirement when the time comes.

19. KEN DAHLBERG

- Bet on your skills.
- Innovate to meet basic human needs.
- Stay open to timely opportunities.
- Use high tech to maintain high touch.
- Do it yourself, but not by yourself.
- Surround yourself with experience.
- Order your priorities around personal faith.
- Decide to do good as part of doing business.
- Keep dreaming, but stay awake.

20. DAVID V. CAVAN

- Expect some explosions in the minefield of life.
- Refuse to become a victim.
- Do all you can and trust God for the rest.
- Get the best advice, then follow your heart.
- Focus on what really matters in life.
- Let trials drive you toward God, not away from him.
- Help others with what you've learned.

NOTES

Chapter 1, "Billion-Dollar Maxims"

1. Walter Wriston, quoted in *Wired,* January 1998.

2. *No-Load Fund Analyst,* June 1995.

3. Arthur Friedman, quoted in Zig Ziglar, *Over the Top* (Nashville: Thomas Nelson, 1997), 80.

4. Joel Arthur Barker, *Future Edge* (New York: William Morrow, 1992), 108.

5. Todd Wilkenson, "Flight of the Lone Eagles," *Jackson Hole Magazine,* Summer/Fall 1996.

6. Dave Berry, *Claw Your Way to the Top* (Emmaus, Pa.: Rodale Press, 1986), 25.

7. *7 Habits of Highly Effective People* Calendar, Stephen Covey.

8. John Stapleford, quoted by Charles P. Wilson, *Business,* May 1994.

9. As quoted by Bill D'Alonzo, source unknown.

Chapter 2, "Beyond Success to Significance"

1. Harriet Rubin, "Peter's Principles," *Inc.,* March 1998.

2. Gregg Levoy, *Callings, Finding and Following an Authentic Life* (New York: Harmony Books, 1997), 151.

3. Ibid., 31.

4. Bob Buford, *Game Plan* (Grand Rapids: Zondervan, 1997), 56–57.

5. Levoy, 311.

Chapter 3, "It Can Be Done!"

1. *7 Habits of Highly Effective People* Calendar, Stephen Covey.

2. Ivor Davis, "Patriot Gains," *Success,* May 1998.

3. Lark Ellen Gould, "Making Money by Selling Inbound," *Travel Agent*, 17 June 1996.

4. ATI press release.

Chapter 4, "MVP"

1. Billy Joel's *Greatest Hits III* video.

2. "Pitching 100 MPH in Phoenix," Ronald Grover, *Business Week*, 30 March 1998.

3. Quoted in Hugh Rawson, *Unwritten Laws: The Unofficial Rules of Life* (New York: Crown Publisher, 1997), 202.

4. Ed Graney, "The Desert Fox," *San Diego Union Tribune*, 15 May 1995.

5. Garry Wills, *Certain Trumpets: the Call of Leadership* (New York: Simon & Schuster, 1994), 189–90.

6. Pat Jordan, "Here's the Windup, and the Pitch," *The New York Times Magazine*, 29 March 1998.

7. Ibid.

8. Ibid.

9. Quoted in Ben Cohen and Jerry Greenfield, *Ben & Jerry's Double Dip, Lead with Your Values and Make Money, Too* (New York: Simon & Schuster, 1997), 88.

Chapter 5, "Exceptionally Ordinary"

1. Donna Hemmila, "Western's Success Not Temporary," *San Francisco Business Times Fast Track Quarterly*, 3–9 October 1997.

2. Ibid.

3. Ben Cohen and Jerry Greenfield, *Ben & Jerry's Double Dip: Lead with Your Values and Make Money, Too* (New York: Simon & Schuster, 1997, 44–45.

4. David Steindll-Rast, *The Music of Silence* (San Francisco: HarperCollins, 1995), 59.

5. Hemmila, "Western's Success Not Temporary."

6. Howard Gardner, *Leading Minds, an Anatomy of Leadership* (New York: Basic Books, 1996), 199.

Chapter 6, "Food for Thought"

1. Howard Schultz, *Pour Your Heart Into It* (New York: Hyperion, 1997), 274.

2. Herman Cain, *Leadership Is Common Sense* (New York: Van Nostrand Reinhold, 1997), 10.

3. "Cain: Leadership is Common Sense," *Nebraska Municipal Review*, October 1997.

4. Wallace Terry, "I Chose to Change My Life," *Parade Magazine*, 13 October 1996.

5. Trevor Meers, "The Hermanator," *New Man*, January/February 1998.

6. Cain, 82.

7. Ibid., 27.

8. Evan Gahr, "Spirited Enterprise," *The American Enterprise*, July/August 1997.

Chapter 7, "Recharged!"

1. Jim Collins, "The Foundation for Doing Good," *Inc.*, December 1997.

2. Dan McGraw, "The Rise of the Christian Capitalists," *U.S. News & World Report*, 13 March 1995.

3. Ben Cohen and Jerry Greenfield, *Ben & Jerry's Double Dip, Lead with Your Values and Make Money, Too* (New York: Simon & Schuster, 1997), 51–52.

4. C. William Pollard, *The Soul of the Firm* (New York: HarperCollins, 1996), 18–21.

5. *7 Habits of Highly Effective People* Calendar, Stephen Covey.

6. Mark 8:36–37.

7. Jerry Seinfeld, *Sein Language* (New York: Bantam Books, 1995), 153.

Chapter 8, "Mastering Your Craft"

1. Quoted in Kevin McCarthy, *The On-Purpose Person* (Colorado Springs: Pinion Press, 1992), 135.

2. Steve Tsuchiyama, "In Search of Buried Talents," *Administrative Radiology Journal*, September 1990.

3. Scott Adams, *The Dilbert Future* (New York: HarperBusiness, 1997), 119–20.

4. Testimonial letter by Jim Zorn.

Chapter 9, "Kid Stuff"

1. As quoted in Henry Adams, *The Education of Henry Adams*, chapter 12.

2. Rosemary Jordano, "Much is at stake in child-care summit," *Boston Globe*, 7 October 1997.

3. Richard Winter, "This Generation Means Business," *Reader's Digest*, October 1997.

4. Paul Hawken, *Growing a Business* (New York: Simon & Schuster, 1997), 19.

5. Ibid., 61.

6. Rosemary Jordano and Marie Oates, "Putting the Children First," *The New York Times*, 9 November 1997.

7. Nancy Rivera Brooks, "Security Blanket," *Los Angeles Times*, 5 December 1995.

8. Robert Coles, *The Moral Intelligence of Children* (New York: PLUME, 1998), 5.

Chapter 10, "Franchising Your Future"

1. Michael F. Gerber, *The E-Myth Revisited: Why Most Small Businesses Don't Work and What to Do About It* (New York: HarperBusiness, 1995), 83.

2. Ibid., 96.

3. Ibid., 2, 82.

4. James H. Amos Jr., *Focus or Failure: America at the Crossroads, Where Are You?* (Mechanicsburg, Pa.: Executive Books, 1998), 57.

5. James C. Collins and Jerry I. Porras, *Built to Last* (New York: HarperBusiness, 1994), 222.

6. John Chambers, "The Next Net," quoted by Jeffrey S. Young in *Wired*, April 1999, 188.

7. Matthew 6:14–15.

8. Amos, 92.

Chapter 11, "Virtual Reality"

1. "The State of the Planet," *Wired*, January 1998.

2. Quoted in Jeffrey Rodengen, *The MicroAge Way* (Fort Lauderdale, Fla.: Write Stuff Enterprises, 1996), 16.

3. Richard Winter, "This Generation Means Business," *Readers' Digest*, October 1997.

4. Tom Peters, *The Tom Peters Seminar: Crazy Times Call for Crazy Organizations* (New York: Vintage Books, 1994), 35.

5. "The Big Payoff," *Success*, April 1998, 54.

6. Rodengen, 91.

7. Excerpted from Frank Toney, *Religious Practices: Their Impact on Wealth Accumulation, Happiness and Health* (forthcoming).

8. Quoted in Herman Cain, *Leadership Is Common Sense* (New York: Van Nostrand Reinhold, 1997), 99.

9. Rodengen, 19.

10. Sinbad, *Sinbad's Guide to Life: Because I Know Everything,* (New York: Bantam Books, 1998), 49.

Chapter 12, "When Life Hands You a Chicken, Make a Sandwich"

1. S. Truett Cathy, *It's Easier to Succeed Than to Fail* (Nashville: Thomas Nelson, 1989), 33.

2. Lea Davis Paul, "Why This Man Doesn't Need Franchising," *QSR*, November/December 1997.

3. Furman Bisher, "Fifty Years of Building a Good Name," 1996, Chick-Fil-A.

4. Joshua Quittner, "Netscape's Survival Kit," *Wired*, April 1998, 157.

5. Zig Ziglar, *Over the Top* (Nashville: Thomas Nelson, 1997), 176.

6. Kevin Salwen, "How Chick-fil-A Hatched New Restaurant Design," *Wall Street Journal, Southeast Journal*, 29 October 1997.

7. Dan McGraw, "The Rise of the Christian Capitalists," *U.S. News & World Report*, 13 March 1995.

8. Jerry Winans, "God's Family Means Business," *Stand Firm*, November 1996.

Chapter 13, "The Road to an IPO"

1. From the TV special "The Life and Times of Ray Stevens."

2. Peter L. Bernstein, *Against the Gods, The Remarkable Story of Risk* (New York: John Wiley & Sons, 1996), 197.

3. Ben Cohen and Jerry Greenfield, *Ben & Jerry's Double Dip: Lead with Your Values and Make Money, Too* (New York: Simon & Schuster, 1997), 92.

4. Kenneth S. Kantzer, *Christianity Today*, 12 May 1989, 40.

Chapter 14, "In Search of Truth"
1. Bill Orr, CEO of Garrett Turbine Company.

2. Rudyard Kipling, "If."

3. Ashleigh Brilliant, *I Have Abandoned My Search for Truth, and Am Now Looking for a Good Fantasy* (Santa Barbara: Woodbridge Press, 1991).

Chapter 15, "Diamonds in the Rough"
1. Quoted in Kevin W. McCarthy, *The On-Purpose Person* (Colorado Springs: Pinion Press, 1992), 117.

2. Michael Porter and Anne Habiby, "A Window on the New Economy," *Inc.*, May 1999, 49–50.

3. C. William Pollard, *The Soul of the Firm* (New York: HarperBusiness, 1996), 113.

4. Howard Schultz, *Pour Your Heart Into It* (New York: Hyperion, 1997), 152.

Chapter 16, "Public Service"
1. Dallas Willard, *The Spirit of the Disciplines* (New York: HarperCollins, 1988), 214.

2. Paul Hawken, *Growing a Business* (New York: Simon & Schuster, 1997), 19.

3. Robert Bork, *Slouching Toward Gomorrah* (New York: HarperCollins, 1997), 336.

4. Zig Ziglar, *Over the Top* (Nashville: Thomas Nelson, 1997), 91.

Chapter 17, "¡La Familia Buena!"
1. Edmund Burke, *Reflections on the Revolutions in France* (1790).

2. Michael E. Thirkill, "Education Spurs Rapid Climb of Young Executives, *Albuquerque Journal*, 28 January 1985.

3. Alvin Tofler, *Powershift: Knowledge, Wealth, and Violence at the Edge of the 21st Century* (New York: Bantam Books, 1991), 182.

4. Albert Einstein, http://stripe.colorado.edu/~judy/einstein/education.html

5. *Que Cards*, a set of fifty-two sayings, published by Leadership Catalyst Inc., Phoenix, 1998.

6. Quoted in Ben Cohen and Jerry Greenfield, B*en & Jerry's Double Dip: Lead with Your Values and Make Money, Too* (New York: Simon & Schuster, 1997), 238–39.

Chapter 18, "Web of Life"

1. From the closing scene in the movie *Mr. Holland's Opus.*

2. Andrew A. Rooney, *Sweet & Sour* (Old Tappan, N.J.: Thorndike Press, 1993), 241–42.

3. Zig Ziglar, *Over the Top* (Nashville: Thomas Nelson, 1997), 224.

4. Letter to Robert A. Fulton on the twentieth anniversary of the founding of Web Industries.

5. Garry Wills, *Certain Trumpets: the Call of Leadership* (New York: Simon & Schuster, 1994), 17–18.

6. Leslie Brokaw, "Books That Transform Companies," *Inc.,* July 1991.

7. Letter to Robert A. Fulton.

8. Don Boroughs, "The Bottom Line on Ethics," *U.S. News & World Report*, 20 March 1995.

9. *The ESOP Report,* August 1993.

10. Howard Gardner, ed., *Leading Minds: An Anatomy of Leadership* (New York: Basic Books, 1996), 178.

Chapter 19, "Where's the Action?"

1. Benjamin Spock and Michael B. Rothanberg, *Dr. Spock's Baby and Child Care,* 6th ed. (New York: Pocket Books, 1992).

2. Joe Foss and Matthew Brennan, *Top Guns* (New York: Pocket Books, 1991), 181.

3. Howard Gardner, ed., *Leading Minds: An Anatomy of Leadership* (New York: Basic Books, 1996), 33.

4. Max Beerbohm, "From Bloomsbury to Baywater," *Mainly on the Air,* 1946.

5. D. J. Tice, *Saint Paul Pioneer Press Express,* 1 February 1998.

6. Quoted in Hugh Rawson, *Unwritten Laws: The Unofficial Rules of Life* (New York: Crown Publisher, 1997), 39.

7. Harvey Mackay, *Swim with the Sharks: Without Being Eaten Alive* (New York: Ballantine Books, 1996), 178.

8. Foss and Brennan, 181.

Chapter 20, "Back from the Brink"

1. Quoted in *Topical Encyclopedia of Living Quotations* (Minneapolis: Bethany House, 1982), 32.

2. Michael F. Gerber, *The E-Myth Revisited: Why Most Small Businesses Don't Work and What to Do About It* (New York: HarperBusiness, 1995), 2.

3. The American Bankruptcy Institute, http://www.abiworld.org/stats/newstatsfront.html

4. Charles Swindoll quoted in Zig Ziglar, *Over the Top* (Nashville: Thomas Nelson, Nashville, 1997), 132.

5. W. Purkiser, quoted in *Topical Encyclopedia of Living Quotations* (Minneapolis, Bethany House, 1982), 244.